TON

UP!

PAUL d'ORLÉANS

A CENTURY OF CAFÉ
RACER SPEED AND STYLE

motorbooks

© 2020 Quarto Publishing Group USA Inc.

Text © 2020 Paul D'Orléans

First Published in 2020 by Motorbooks, an imprint of The Quarto Group, 100 Cummings Center, Suite 265-D, Beverly, MA 01915, USA.

T (978) 282-9590 F (978) 283-2742 QuartoKnows.com

Motorbooks titles are also available at discount for retail, wholesale, promotional, and bulk purchase. For details, contact the Special Sales Manager by email at specialsales@quarto.com or by mail at The Quarto Group, Attn: Special Sales Manager, 100 Cummings Center, Suite 265-D, Beverly, MA 01915, USA.

24 23 22 21 20   1 2 3 4 5

ISBN: 978-0-7603-6045-3

Digital edition published in 2019

eISBN: 978-0-7603-4046-0

Library of Congress Cataloging-in-Publication Data

Names: D'Orléans, Paul, author.
Title: Ton up! : a century of café racer speed and style / Paul d'Orléans.
Description: Beverly, Massachusetts : Motorbooks, 2019. | Includes index.
Identifiers: LCCN 2019029864| ISBN 9780760360453 (Hardcover) | ISBN
    9780760360460 (eBook)
Subjects: LCSH: Motorcycles--Customizing--History. | Motorcycles,
    Racing--Pictorial works. | Subculture--Great Britain--History--20th
    century.
Classification: LCC TL442.7 .D67 2019 | DDC 629.227/50941--dc23 LC record available at
https://lccn.loc.gov/2019029864

Cover and Interior design by Faceout Studio
Title page photo: Ben Part
Front case photo: Ken Takayanagi
Back case photo: Phillip Tooth
Front endpaper photo: The Vintagent
Back endpaper photo: Hockenheim Museum Archive

CONTENTS

FOREWORD

For the past hundred years, motorcycles have been the black sheep of the transportation family. They eschew the safety of the automobile, the cargo capacity of the bus, and the efficiency of the subway. Instead they expose their riders to danger and the ferocity of the elements.

Lip service is paid to practicality and reliability, but as we all know, the primary appeal of the motorcycle comes from acceleration and velocity. The average two-wheeler is far, far quicker than the average car; as early as 1925, the Brough Superior was capable of nudging "the Ton."

This book unravels the story of that search for speed and its pinnacle in the café racer movement. Since the 1920s, riders have been stripping down and modifying their bikes, but the craze only really entered public consciousness in England in the 1960s.

Triumphs, Nortons, and BSAs became synonymous with the café racer scene, zooming between coffee shops on the outskirts of London. Yes, the historical details of this era have been endlessly debated, often by persons wearing rose-tinted spectacles and leather jackets festooned with patches. But everyone agrees that the first café racer era was a pivotal moment in motorcycle history.

It faded quickly. By the 1980s, extreme speeds were available to all thanks to the emergence of liter-class Japanese superbikes. The "racer on the road" was commonplace, and even the most highly tuned machine from the 1960s would lose the traffic light Grand Prix to a showroom stock 600cc sportbike.

Then in 2008 something interesting started to happen. Global interest in the traditional café racer style perked up again. Custom bike builders started to drift away from blinged-out choppers and look for old Brit iron

and BMW airheads to rip apart. Factory designers began to add traditional styling cues, ribbed seats, and spoked wheels to new models. And by 2016, café racers were once again everywhere.

If there's anyone qualified to examine this colorful corner of two-wheeled history, it's Paul d'Orléans. In *Ton Up*, America's preeminent motorcycle historian takes us on a wild ride from the earliest days of converted bicycles to the internet-fueled "alt-moto" craze of recent years.

Buckle up and enjoy the ride.

Chris H.

CHRIS HUNTER
FOUNDER, BIKE EXIF

PREFACE

This book represents a lifelong passion of its author, whose interest in café racers began in the summer of 1984. I'd learned to ride in 1978 on small utilitarian Hondas, but after university, my friend Jim Gilman transmitted his vintage-moto virus by offering rides on his 1956 BMW R50 and handing over a milk crate stuffed with *Classic Bike* and *The Classic Motorcycle* magazines. I devoured those magazines, wore them thin and foxed their edges until the staples no longer held. While my first big bikes were vintage BMWs, an R60/2 and a single-cylinder R26, within a year I replaced both with a 1966 Norton Atlas. The siren song of 1950s and '60s café racers had captured me, and I bought my first leather "biker" jacket; my riding kit also included a vintage silver jet helmet and Stadium goggles, finished out with a white T-shirt, cuffed Levi's, and eight-hole Doc Martens boots. I had been a punk, and became a punk/rocker, and I was not alone among my friends: Adam Fisher also found a Norton Atlas, and Bill Charman his Velocette MSS.

Older British bikes had a renaissance with young San Francisco riders in the 1980s, as they were inexpensive and had tremendous style. Unlike the rockers of the '60s, we congregated at bars in the evenings, with a nightly lineup of vintage Triumphs, Nortons, BMWs, and Velocettes. Adam and I attracted other Norton enthusiasts and created a café racer club, the Roadholders, while other friends formed the British Death Fleet, named for a Falklands war headline. Our dedication to the rocker aesthetic led to Adam's 1987 revival of the Ace Café in San Francisco, a chic rehabbed industrial space with locally fabricated Philippe Starck–knockoff steel chairs (welders were our constant friends) and an enormous vintage motorcycle poster in the entry. We weren't working-class greasers; we were postpunk art-school graduates who loved the café racer style of the year we were born.

In subsequent decades, I collected literature to feed my insatiable passion for old motorcycles. Hundreds of models passed through my garage, mostly café racers of the 1920s through 1970s. Plastic-covered motorcycles of the 1980s rarely excited my interest as a student of both design and history, and multicylinder Japanese engines seemed soulless. I considered the last aesthetic masterpiece of engine design to be Fabio Taglioni's magnificent Ducati round-case 750GT. In a case of "looks right, is right," my own 750GT was amazingly reliable, as proven on one 6,000-mile solo journey exploring mountainous roads up the West Coast of the United States and down the spine of the Rockies to the Southwest.

My main squeeze, though, was my British racing green 1966 Velocette-Thruxton, which was my sole transport in 1989 and grew into an extension of my senses. The Thruxton was built to satisfy the requirements of a rider exactly like me, who demanded tremendous style, world championship–bred competence on the road, and the ability to deliver hours-on-end ton-up riding without calamity. The publication of this book marks the thirtieth year of our acquaintance and, thus, is something of an homage to "Courgette" and all the other incredibly stylish café racers I've owned over the years, photos of which are spread throughout the pages that follow. May these words and photos inspire you in the way café racers have inspired me, led to my deepest friendships, and shaped my preference for the twisty bits on life's road.

Veloce Ltd. director Bertie Goodman rode, raced, and broke records on his family product: Velocette motorcycles. For their 1962 catalog he's flat out, testing a 1961 Venom Clubman at 106 miles per hour. *TV*

INTRODUCTION: THE NEED FOR SPEED AND THE CAFÉ RACER IMPULSE

The culture of youthful, reckless speed did not begin with the motorcycle. The fastest travel for thousands of years was the horse, and subcultures of fast horsemen populate the folk tales of many societies. A fast horse was a point of tremendous pride and identity for its rider, and like-minded riders affected styles of dress and speech peculiar to their inclinations. Reckless young riders were decried as hooligans, and the preening, fashion-conscious speed lover was never a beloved figure except in envious condemnation.

Mat Oxley mentions such trends in his excellent book *Speed: The One Genuinely Modern Pleasure*, with riders adopting particular fashions and modes of speech as spice for their lust for speed on public roads: "At the height of the Georgian era, less than a century before the internal combustion engine exploded onto the scene, Britain's wealthy ne'er do wells sought ever more decadent ways in which to fritter away their riches on thrill seeking. The Four Horse Club was established in the early nineteenth century by a bunch of mad, bad aristocrats who enjoyed racing each other in their horsedrawn carriages. . . . They were so keen to appear genuine that they learned to *eff* and *blind* like their servants. One member of the Four Horse Club had several teeth removed, so he could spit like a grizzled coachman as he charged around the streets like the world's first joyrider."

Parallels to café racer subcultures on wheels can be seen with the first pedal cycles. It took until 1869 for pedals to appear on the bicycle (or velocipede), a bright idea credited both to André Michaux and Pierre Lallement, whose idea was apparently inspired by the pedal-driven stone wheels of itinerant knife sharpeners. The Michaux bicycle had pedal cranks directly attached to the front axle, with footrests above the front wheel for coasting. As pneumatic tires would not be invented for twenty years, these bicycles deserved their nickname of "boneshaker," although their saddles were fixed to tempered steel springs, which helped over bumps. The first velocipedes were also called dandy horses, as fancy young men were their most enthusiastic adherents. The author of 1869's of "A Two-Wheeled Steed," who was undoubtedly such a dandy, gave the first exposition in English on the joys of speed on two wheels:

In 1869 the rider of this Michaux "Dandy Horse" was the prototypical fan of the racer on the road—cocky, proud of his wheels, and dressed to impress. *TV*

> *[The pedal-cycle] came into public notoriety at the last French International Exhibition, from which time the rage for them has gradually developed itself, until in this present 1869, it may be said that Paris has been driven mad on velocipedes . . . The two-wheeler, when on the turn, stands at an inclination like a skater's body, more or less acute according to the quickness of the curve to be described. The slightly increased labour of climbing a hill is nothing to the zest imparted by a knowledge that there is sure to be a hill the other side to go down, and that is the most luxurious travelling that can be imagined. Descending an incline at full speed, balanced on a beautifully tempered steel spring that takes every jolt from the road—wheels spinning over the ground so lightly they scarce seem to touch it—the driver's legs rested comfortably on the cross-bar in front—shooting the hill at a speed of thirty or forty miles an hour—the sensation is only comparable to that of flying, and is worth all the pains it costs in learning to experience it.*

That "sensation of flying" is familiar to anyone on a motorcycle. Speed inspired the idea of adding a motor to the pedal-cycle, to extend that feeling indefinitely.

SYLVESTER H. ROPER AND THE LUST FOR SPEED

In 1869, Sylvester H. Roper built a steam-powered boneshaker, which was well known around Boston and demonstrated at fairs, but motorcycles saw little further development until the invention of both the safety bicycle and the inflatable tire in 1895. That year, Roper was commissioned by

Albert Pope to build a steam pacer for his Columbia bicycle racing team. It was a peak year for the nineteenth-century bicycle boom, which had knock-on effects for Western culture, including the ideas that governments should finance infrastructure (roads) and that women should be free to move about—and, ultimately, vote, which took another generation.

While machines like the Hildebrand & Wolfmüller in Germany (1894) and the Holden Four in England (1897) were among the earliest production motorcycles, their design relied on locomotive engineering, with the rear wheel directly linked to the engine's connecting rods. They were not freewheeling or swift, and that branch of development was soon abandoned. Motorizing the safety bicycle proved a better idea, and the accumulated design wisdom of the bicycle industry was absorbed into the motorcycle's DNA. The first widely seen motorcycles were cycle pacers for racing: a motorized (steam, electric, or gas-powered) pacing cycle allowed

A sporting champion on two and four wheels, Giosué Giuppone raced for Peugeot on monsters like this 1905 12-horsepower track bike weighing 110 pounds. *AC*

LES SPORTS. — MOTOCYCLETTISTE ITALIEN
GIUPPONE

velodrome racers in the United States and Europe to draft motorcycles to reach thrilling speeds. Crowds flocked to see the first motorized vehicles of their lives; the pacers had become the action, and it was natural that these pioneering motorcyclists began racing one another on velodromes.

Thus, in 1895, Pope supplied a heavyweight Columbia safety bicycle to Sylvester Roper, who added a compact steam engine of his own design, and it proved a fine road machine. Roper rode his second "self-propeller" regularly from his workshop in Roxbury to the Boston Yacht Club, at the time about 7 miles away—the range of his fuel and water supply. Roper loved demonstrating his speed on Boston's roads and at fairs, enjoying a reputation as the fastest thing on wheels, able to, as he said, "climb any hill and outrun any horse." He was invited to demonstrate his steamer at the Charles River Speedway, a banked wooden velodrome in Boston's Allston neighborhood, on June 1, 1896, when he was seventy-three. He blew off the nation's fastest bicycle racers, so track officials urged him to unleash the hissing beast, and the septuagenarian inventor was excited to explore its performance. After a few scorching 40-mile-per-hour laps, Roper was seen to wobble into the arms of his son, Charles, where he collapsed, dead. Roper likely had a heart attack from the thrill of speed and became the first motorcycle fatality. He may or may not have built the first functional motorcycle, but he was definitely our first speed demon and first martyr to the gods of speed.

The racing crouch began on the backs of horses, evolved in 1800s bicycle racing, and continued with motorcycles like this 1903 Phoenix. *TV*

DANCING WITH THE LAW

The urge for speed is as old as humankind, and so, unfortunately, is the urge to regulate speed using the force of law. No speed limits for horses are recorded in deep antiquity, but "reckless" riding was commented on. It wasn't until 1419 that common-sense speed limits were legally enacted in the *Liber Albus,* the first book of English common law by John Carpenter, the town clerk of London: "No carter within the liberties shall drive his cart more quickly when it is unloaded, than when it is loaded; for the

Get down to it! The eternal pose of the racer on the road, as seen with this fellow on a very early Harley-Davidson single-cylinder model. *TV*

avoiding of divers perils and grievances, under pain of paying forty pence unto the Chamber, and of having his body committed to prison at the will of the Mayor."

The next published speed limits appeared in 1652 in New Amsterdam (later called New York), where it was decreed, "No Wagons, Carts, or Sleighs shall be run, rode or driven at a gallop," otherwise one risked a fine of two Flemish pounds (about $150 today). The English enacted speed limits with the United Kingdom Stage Carriage Act of 1832, which made it unlawful to endanger the safety of (presumably commercial) carriage passengers by "furious driving." Numerical speed limits were laid down in that country in a series of Locomotive Acts between 1861 and 1878, first with an overall 10-mile-per-hour limit, then 2 miles per hour in towns and 4 in the country-side by 1865, with the requirement that "road locomotives" (i.e., steam cars and omnibuses) be preceded by a man with a red flag. The 1896 Locomotives on Highways Act raised the legal limit to a wild 14 miles per hour, which was considered the equal of "furious driving" on a horse and was greeted with jubilation by pioneer automobilists and motorcyclists alike. They celebrated with an organized run from London to Brighton Pier, which is repeated annually as the Pioneer Run.

The first speed limit in the United States was in Connecticut, which in 1901 mandated maximums of 12 miles per hour in the city and 15 in the country, proving that New Englanders are even more uptight than the English themselves. As much early motorcycle racing in the United States was conducted on the road, Connecticut was to be avoided—although New York, despite its seventeenth-century speed-trap roots, was the site of many endurance contests from the earliest years and saw several speed records set at over 60 miles per hour before 1910 by the likes of Glenn H. Curtiss.

The Hell Rider and the Happy Hooligan

Glenn H. Curtiss, who caught the racing bug on bicycles in the late 1890s, was described in *Time* as having an "appetite for speed that has always been insatiable." He built his first motorcycle in 1901, wanting to go faster than pedals would allow, and dubbed it the "Happy Hooligan." He spent happy hours buzzing Hammondsport, New York, at full throttle; by January 1902 he had built two more machines, with heavier chassis and engines of his own design that used ball bearings instead of plain bushings, which proved as fast as anything else built in the United States. His first motorcycle race was May 1902 with the NY Motor Cycle Club, but he "only" made second and third place against the slightly faster Indians. That inspired Curtiss to create a new design for the 1903 NYMCC race—America's first V-twin engine—and he trounced the competition. That same day, he headed to Yonkers for the National Cycle Association race at the Empire Track, where he beat all comers in a 10-mile race, then recorded a mile lap at 63.4 miles per hour, which made him both the American motorcycle champion and the fastest motorcyclist in the world.

Curtiss's motorcycle skills earned him the name Hell-Rider, and speed was his North Star. His motors were the best in the industry, which is why Tom Baldwin, America's first dirigible builder/pilot, used Curtiss engines exclusively—a habit shared with other pioneering aviators. Two dirigible builders asked for a lightweight V-8 motor in 1906, and Curtiss designed one with 40 horsepower: it purred in a way his twins never did, so

he instructed his team to build a motorcycle chassis around it! The finished beast was over 7 feet long, and Curtiss had to sit over the rear wheel, as he could not straddle the motor.

In January 1907, Curtiss took his V-8 monster to Ormond Beach, Florida, where he first set a new world speed record of 77.58 miles per hour with his twin-cylinder motorcycle. At day's end, an enormous crowd lined the beach to watch him ride the beast. Wearing a leather suit and a helmet of his own design, he strapped himself to his motorcycle, fearful of being blown off by the wind at top speed. Multiple stopwatches recorded his measured mile at 26.4 seconds, or 136.6 miles per hour, which made him the fastest human in the world. On a return run, his driveshaft broke and flailed wildly, and it took all of Curtiss's skills to bring the machine safely to a halt. It took twenty-four years for another motorcycle to match his speed. Meanwhile, Curtiss said the ride had satisfied something inside him, so he switched to making aircraft!

Ernst Neumann was a German artist living in Paris who later built Neander motorcycles. Here he rides a 1904 Griffon V-twin in an amazing fur coat. *TT*

THE SCENE OF THE CLIMB: ILLEGAL STREET RACING IN THE 1900S

The United Kingdom was saddled from 1903 with a blanket 20-mile-per-hour speed limit, which was abolished only in 1930. Thus, unless a rider was on private property or in a closed park (such as Crystal Palace in London), any hillclimb, speed test, or point-to-point contest was illegal. Nevertheless, they happened frequently! Magazines like *The Motor Cycle* (est. 1903) reported dozens of contests annually, organized by the Motor Cycle Club (MCC) and its local branches. Clubs went to great pains to either secure support of the local constabulary or scrupulously conceal the location of races, even from the competitors, until the hour of the event:

"The MCC committee had been wise enough to keep the position of the hill up which the competition was to take place a profound secret . . . all the competitors who arrived at the Old Salisbury Hotel . . . knew nothing beyond the fact that the scene of the climb was within a few miles of the meeting place. . . . [Still], the sight of a policeman or two, and an inspector, compelled nearly everyone to dismount and ask if they were there to aid or hinder the interests of motor cycling, and one bold man who asked the inspector why he was there was politely told that it was to time every rider, and to issue a summons to every one who exceeded twenty miles per hour."

The Automobile Association (AA) had scouts set up across the country to warn motorists of police speed traps, which were common outside of towns. Policemen relished the opportunity to levy fines on riders, and the AA scouts were much praised for their service. They were so effective that, under the heading of "Frustrating Crime?," an editor of *The Motor Cycle* noted that "a policeman was actually seen crawling on his hands and knees over Paines Hill bridge, Cobham, in order to evade them." This widespread disrespect of the law by otherwise respectable (and relatively wealthy) motorcyclists was seen as undermining the pillars of civilized society and breeding contempt for the police. The flurry of letters each spring from outraged bikers caught in speed traps would echo ever after for fast riders. Of course, when the blanket speed limit was abolished in 1930, riders seeking the outer limits of motorcycle performance on the road were labeled hooligans!

1907: THE ISLE OF MAN TT

As racing was impossible on British roads, the Europeans hosted Grands Prix and International Cup races, first in France and Germany. This galled the nascent British motorcycle industry, which was anxious to prove the worth of its machines without the trade-supported races and notorious dirty tricks of continental events. A solution was found in the Isle of Man, whose thousand-year-old independent parliament did not abide by British speed laws. When the first Tourist Trophy (TT) race

Alfred Dunhill Ltd. offered quality motoring gear from 1893. A cheeky disdain for the police was typical of their advertising in the early years. *TV*

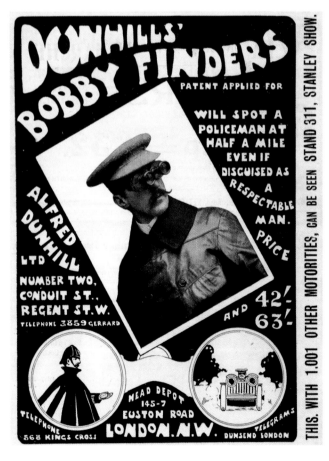

The Futurists

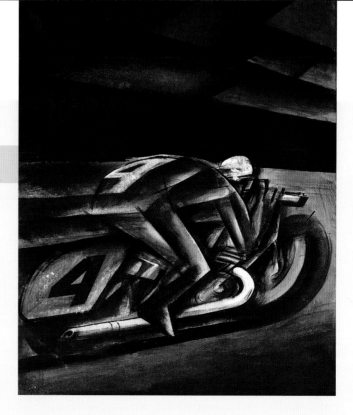

"We are on the extreme promontory of the centuries! What is the use of looking behind at the moment when we must open the mysterious shutters of the impossible? Time and Space died yesterday. We are already living in the absolute, since we have already created eternal, omnipresent Speed."

Futurism was the Italian art movement founded in 1909 by Filippo Marinetti, known as the "caffeine of Europe" for his excited devotion to speed, noise, machinery, youth, and violence. His Futurist Manifesto was front-page news in 1909, an outrageous tract with implications far beyond art—as shocking and threatening as a ransom note. It was the first modern art manifesto and the kind of writing that landed authors in jail, with its exhortations to violence and rejection of old ways of seeing things: "We declare that the splendor of the world has been enriched by a new beauty: the beauty of speed. A racing automobile with its bonnet adorned with great tubes like serpents with explosive breath . . . a roaring motorcar that seems to run on machine-gun fire, is more beautiful than the Victory of Samothrace."

Despite their barmy antics with chaotic live performances and absurdist sound poetry, the futurists accurately foresaw an individually mobilized society, in which barriers of distance and dialect would be eradicated and the whole world within reach. Futurism was the only modern art movement to embrace motorcycles decades before their on-road performance matched their artistic value. Its followers loved bikes for what they symbolized, and while their near-hysterical adulation of clunky 1909 bikes now seems quaint, they understood the implications of new technology. As poets, painters, sculptors, and performance artists, they broke all the rules, scattering words across the page (Marinetti called them "words in freedom"), invented sound

poetry to imitate city noises, and created a new visual language to express speed and energy. The futurists invented modern art, graphic design, poetry, film, and theater. Painters such as Fortunato Depero and Ivo Pannaggi loved fast motorcycles, as did "aeropoet" Bruno Giordano Sanzin, who wrote "In the Arms of Speed the Goddess" in 1924:

The motorcycle jumps, then intoxicated with joy, hurls quivering on the dusty road. I run and run, but I never seem to be fast enough, and I want to increase speed by angrily pushing on the lever. The machine restores its strength and doubles its speed. Now wheels don't touch the ground anymore: they fly, and fly . . .

The futurists found new ways to capture movement in art and words and graphics, and their aesthetic impact rippled around the world. Graphic artists took note, and gradually the fussy late-1800s Beaux-Arts advertising posters featuring busty corseted goddesses floating on clouds over motorcycles gave way to speed whiskers, urgent movement, and the adrenaline romance of Speed. Big-breasted goddesses would return to advertising, but not until the late 1960s!

was run in 1907, there were single- and twin-cylinder classes, won by Charlie Collier on a Matchless and Rem Fowler on a Peugeot-engined Norton, respectively. The course was a rural farm track, totally unpaved barring the cobblestones in Douglas, but it was the start of something big. Manufacturers soon responded with purpose-built racing machines for the event, as well as "TT models" for sale to the public. These were some of the original café racers, built explicitly as racers on the road. Manufacturers were aware that very few TT replicas would ever compete in the TT, or any other race, but they had registered the desires of certain type of rider, who wanted the fastest motorcycle available.

1907: BROOKLANDS OPENS

English car and motorcycle enthusiasts greeted the arrival of the world's first purpose-built motorsports track in 1907 with barely repressed glee, as they'd been saddled with the blanket 20-mile-per-hour speed limit since 1903. Even the upper-crust scions of the auto industry could not be contained on Brooklands's opening day of April 7, 1907, and the parade of fabric-topped Edwardian touring cars slowly gathered speed as the reality sank in with drivers: they were on a racetrack! Canvas tops ballooned, ladies' shawls fluttered, and men's hats puffed skyward like graduation day, which in a sense it was.

The earliest specialized racing models were sold starting around 1905. This 1906 Mars inspired the speed dreams of the first motorcyclists. *HMA*

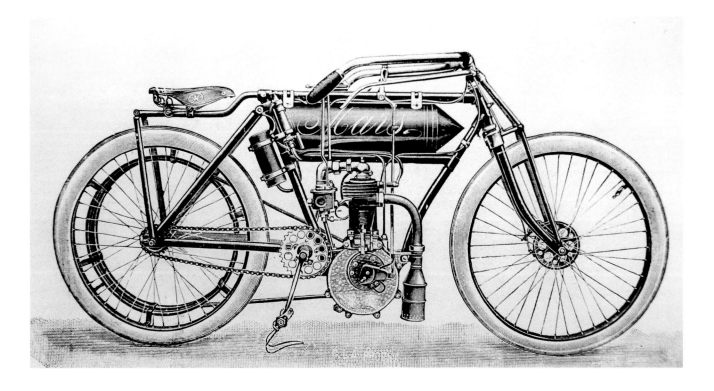

The event was also, in the words of one observer, "perfect pandemonium." The Age of Speed was born that day, with Brooklands its mecca.

The first motorcycle race at Brooklands was between two café racers. Motorcycles were ignored on opening day and wouldn't race officially for another year, but the track was available. As usual, youth got there first: the riders were two Oxford undergraduates, Gordon McMinnies with his Triumph Puffing Billy, and Oscar Bickford on a Vindec Special with a hot Peugeot V-twin motor. It was a match race between friends, who'd convinced clerk of the course Ernst de Rodakowski (known as Roda) to open the gates and witness the affair while the track was officially closed for winter on Tuesday, February 25, 1908. McMinnies won, but he experienced a frightening speed wobble while recording 59.8 miles per hour over the flying half mile. He was awarded the first British Automobile Racing Club certificate for a motorcyclist.

LEFT: With a maximum speed limit of 20 miles per hour, England was a hotbed of police activity. Riders became lawbreakers, and most road trials ended this way. *TV*

BELOW: This 1902 Clément is among the very earliest V-twins with its beautiful narrow-angle motor. The handlebars tell the tale: this is a "racer on the road." *PdO*

Both these machines were road-registered, and Bickford's Vindec Special was the first example of a TT replica of the type beloved ever after by street racers. It was identical to the machines that had taken second and fourth places in the 1907 TT twin-cylinder class. McMinnies's Triumph was a replica of the second- and third-place machines in the TT's single-cylinder class, whose motor would remain in production another thirty-five years. These were among the fastest road bikes available in 1907, and the great argument of the day pitted single-cylinder engines against V-twins for power and reliability. They had been separated at the TT, but Bickford and McMinnies wanted to settle the question for themselves: which was faster? On that day it was the single, and in truth, very few V-twins could beat a single-cylinder bike of the same capacity until that capacity passed 600cc. Then the V-twin, with less stress on its half-sized components, would shine.

THE AMERICAN ABROAD

Indian was the first American company to extend its influence into Europe, supporting forays at the Isle of Man TT and Brooklands starting in 1909. Americans understood the Isle of Man TT to be the toughest motorcycle race in the world. The English believed they built the best and fastest bikes, which was probably true, until Indian standardized a two-speed gearbox and clutch on its all-chain-drive models. Scott's two-strokes had the only other "two-speeder" at the TT, with a two-chain primary drive system. Indian was eager to prove itself, and Oscar Hedstrom, the company's chief designer, sought to increase international sales. It was already the biggest seller in the United States and selling three times as much as its nearest rival in England, Triumph, which only sold a thousand motorcycles in 1909.

The Brooklands speedbowl opened just two weeks after the first TT. Tales of Brooklands's dominant rider, Charlie Collier, and his own-make Matchless motorcycles reached Hedstrom, who noted that Collier's top speeds (around 68 miles per hour) were slower than his Indians. For 1909, Hedstrom created the first factory racing team and shipped two specially modified 750cc racers (the twin-cylinder class limit) for the Isle of Man TT. The race was rough, and while the Matchless of Harry Collier, Charlie's brother, won the twin-cylinder class, Guy Lee Evans was runner-up in Indian's first island foray. The English certainly took note of the vermillion American motorcycle, and Indian sales blossomed in English soil.

From the beginning, factories understood the publicity of speed. In 1907 Indian sent a team to Ormond Beach, Florida, where this V-twin hit 112 miles per hour. *TV*

SELLING SPEED: THE RACER ON THE ROAD

Until the 1930s, a very thin veneer of civility separated actual racing motorcycles from racers on the road. Organized racing created purpose-built racing motorcycles, and manufacturers found a ready market selling race replicas as the apex machines of their model range. Advertisers found a natural hook in the lure of speed, although manufacturers rarely discussed that what certain riders really wanted in their speed-demon souls was the fastest motorcycle available. Since the first days of the twentieth century, builders and buyers of motorcycles have played a complex dance around the subject of speed, with the industry cloaking itself in respectability and keeping a low profile about the exhilaration of pulling the throttle lever all the way back. Riders were savvy to the game, and they also avoided explicit celebrations of the narcotic draw of speed and its handmaiden, danger.

While manufacturers relied on the excitement of their racers in advertising, it was ancillary suppliers (of tires, chains, magnetos, and so on) who tore the brown paper wrapper from the pornography of speed, glorifying competition and competitors in equal measure. Not being makers of motorcycles themselves, they were free to sell the adrenaline high of splitting the atmosphere at lethal velocities—thus we see ads for Dunlop tires, Lodge spark plugs, and Castrol oil showing a rider flat on the tank, "speed whiskers" streaming behind. The early motorcycle press devoted a huge percentage of its copy to racing, with small, grainy photos

OPPOSITE: The earnest look of this young man on his brand new 1909 Indian V-twin tells the tale. He's primed for a street race with goggles at the ready. *JD*

BELOW: A very early race replica—a 1907 Vindec Special with Peugeot V-twin engine just like the 2nd place winner at the first Isle of Man TT. *TV*

of riders crouched over their machines, kicking up dust on dirt roads. Shorthand tales of neck-and-neck racing stirred the imagination of thousands of "speed bugs" who wanted a piece for themselves. And a successful machine like an Indian or Curtiss, Norton or Vindec Special, held a strong attraction for a rider inclined to speed, wanting his or her own racer on the road.

LEFT: Here we see New York road racing in 1908; A.G. Chappie on an Indian torpedo tank with no protective gear—an ordinary rider at very high speed. *TV*

BELOW: Joe Merkel was a pioneering manufacturer in Milwaukee. This 1909 Merkel has super sports dropped handlebars and an early license plate. *JD*

OPPOSITE: The skull has been attached to motorcycles as *memento mori* and power symbol since the dawn of the century as this 1909 postcard demonstrates. *TV*

THE 1910s: RACERS ON THE ROAD

After a decade of real production, motorcycles turned a corner in the 1910s, becoming more reliable, less likely to catch fire, and easier to ride, although the market for bikes was still small worldwide. In 1911, Indian was the largest motorcycle factory in the world, but produced only about eleven thousand machines. The primary users of motorcycles were still men, but a small percentage of women did ride in many countries By the early teens, the race replica as a category of motorcycle had grown along with the popularity of new racing venues. Riders who preferred fast motorcycles were known as "speed bugs" in the United States, and "speed merchants" in the United Kingdom. The writer known as Ixion of *The Motor Cycle* noted as early as 1911 the growth of interest in fast machines, calling them a "new army of speed merchants: Sprint work has become such a wholesale business of late that quite a fleet of riders know all there is to be known about tuning up any engine one cares to name." As mentioned in the introduction, sprint racing was completely illegal in the United Kingdom, which had a blanket speed limit of 20 miles per hour during the whole of the 1910s and '20s. But that didn't stop riders from speed-tuning their road bikes for road trials organized by their local Motor Cycle Club—under strictest secrecy, of course.

OPPOSITE: The Collier brothers' Matchless motorcycles were kings of early British racing. Here Harry Collier straddles his 1911 overhead-valve V-twin. *HMA*

"THE MACHINE OF TO-DAY IS SUFFICIENTLY PERFECT"

Ixion was the nom de plume of Canon Basil Davies, a guru to three generations of British motorcyclists. In 1911, he declared the products of the British motorcycle industry to be sufficiently perfect "for all practical purposes." Davies had been a motorcyclist since the 1890s, suffering through their early years, when surface carburetors would catch fire, batteries would break, and top-heavy machines would skid: the "dreaded side-slip." By 1910, engines were low in the chassis and robust frames could handle rough treatment, with reliable magneto ignition and carburetors that didn't rely on evaporation to mix air and fuel. While Ixion enjoyed fast riding, he was no tearaway, but British riders generally were ahead of the rest of the world in their wholehearted embrace of the racer on the road. While factories in many countries included race replicas in their catalogs, the sheer number introduced by British brands in the 1910s put them at the head of the trend. "TT" models and their kin sold in numbers far in excess of those entered in the Isle of Man TT: one factory never had more than a handful of their machines entered into an early TT race, but TT models and other race replicas sold in the thousands.

After taking 1-2-3 in the 1911 Isle of Man TT, Indian quickly offered a TT Model, a racing replica intended for road use, complete with full fenders. *TV*

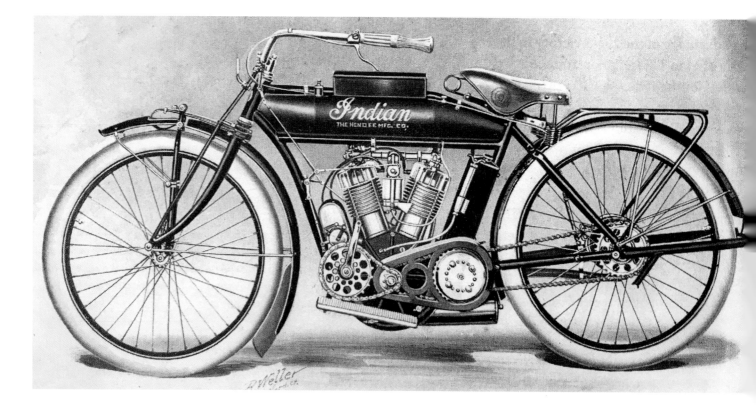

Manufacturers well understood the appeal of a fast motorcycle to the buying public. Race replicas were almost always the range-leading models and those most typically featured in ads, with speed as their selling point. Now that riders could legally indulge in racing on tracks, race victories and speed records were the number-one subjects of motorcycle advertising. Racing and record-breaking were investments for manufacturers, as professional riders kept brands in the news, so manufacturers naturally praised winning racers and boasted of their fine machines. They were careful not to explicitly encourage fast road riding, as that could expose them to claims of irresponsibly supporting illegal activity, but advertising their racing victories in the context of a road motorcycle advertisement was acceptable. Regardless of the fact that only one customer in a thousand might actually take up racing, that one racer, and the mere possibility of racing, provided cover for the whole of the café racer phenomenon.

Many brands sold race replicas, but Norton deserves credit for inventing the factory-built café racer in 1914 with the Brooklands Road Special (BRS). It'd introduced the Brooklands Special racer the year prior, which must have elicited queries about its suitability on the road, but the BRS was advertised as a road bike, although it was almost indistinguishable from the Brooklands Special. Norton's BRS showed a canny self-awareness that the manufacturer's primary customer for "racing" motorcycles was a young rider who preferred private speed contests on public roads, between friends or strangers, to prove who was best at handling their motorcycle. Or customers simply wanted to be seen riding the latest hot model from a famous brand. This made Norton the first in a very long line of manufacturers catering to café racer fans.

Among the hottest British bikes of the teens were Freddie Barnes's Zeniths. Barnes had invented the Gradua variable-ratio belt drive system in 1907, which proved a huge advantage in competitions against single-geared belt-drivers. Graduas were famously banned in many events, as race organizers grew weary of being beaten by machines that could actually climb hills without a running start. Zeniths primarily used J. A Prestwich (JAP) V-twins, were popular with fast riders both on and off the tracks, and had an enviable competition history in the 1920s at Brooklands, where they won more Gold Stars than any

Bursting with speed! The familiar racing crouch and dropped handlebars of a racer on the road are used to advertise Rom Tyres in 1911. *TV*

other make. William Brough, father of racer George Brough, also built twin-cylinder hot rods but preferred flat twins as the ideal layout—and, unlike his son, he built his own engines. Brough was keen on supporting women competitors with specially tuned Ladies Models, which several famous women rode. Female riders vexed the letter writers of the motorcycle magazines, who debated the appropriateness of large-capacity machines for women and had the temerity to suggest which bikes they should ride. That always drew a response from women, who pointed out their paternalistic presumptuousness!

Women riders in England gained particular visibility in the 1910s, entering and doing well in competitions. The first motorcycle events specifically for women were organized in 1911, which was the start of a golden era for women riders in the United Kingdom. Both *The Motor Cycle* and *Motorcycling* inaugurated reports and regular columns written by women, like the Through Feminine Goggles feature in *The Motor Cycle*. Manufacturers catered to female riders with Ladies Models, which used a dipped frame like women's bicycles to accommodate a skirt, although machines like the Scott two-stroke and the Ner-A-Car needed no such modification and were pointedly advertised to women. While many Ladies Models

OPPOSITE: Proving the universality of the racing crouch, this Italian rider on his 1913 Zenith 6 horsepower gets down to it with a very useful Gradua variable belt drive. *TV*

BELOW: Sex on wheels! A hot motorcycle and a snappy outfit are an irresistible combo, as with this young man posing on his 1913 Excelsior 7-C. *CG*

Fast motorcycles stirred global demand; this 1910 Peugeot 7 horsepower Type Y is pictured in Tasmania with its dashing pilot wisely wearing leather jodhpurs. *HMA*

were lightweights, several manufacturers built special large-capacity versions; women riders had a voice in the media, a place in competition, and machines designed to suit their stature. This remarkable period lasted two decades but vanished with the Great Depression, after which women riders also nearly vanished from the motorcycle press, a situation that lasted for the next half century, until the 1980s.

AMERICANS AT HOME AND ABROAD

By the early 1910s, American factories had taken what they could from pioneering European designs such as those from DeDion-Bouton and FN, and created an independent industry with a particular technological flavor. Americans embraced the motorcycle in greater numbers than any other country, and in some ways, the 1910s were peak years for motorcycles in the grand scheme of transport, before the Ford Model T made serious inroads. American manufacturers followed closely what was happening in Europe and began to look abroad to sell more motorcycles, which meant sending racing machines to foreign countries. Many American companies sold racing models in the 1910s, and they were among the most technically advanced motorcycles in the world. Cyclone set an example by selling a road version of its scorching overhead-cam (OHC) V-twin racer from 1915, the most exotic motorcycle ever sold to the public at the time. Indian's amazing eight-valve overhead-valve (OHV) racer appeared in 1911 but was never offered for the road, nor could it in truth be ridden on the road—with no clutch, gears, brakes, or suspension, it was a true track machine. It was a terrific ambassador abroad, as the factory sent eight-valves (and four-valve singles) to race in Britain, France, Australia, and elsewhere. Harley-Davidson followed suit later in the decade when it built its own eight-valve racer, which set speed records in the United States and Australia.

Decades before the Gold Star, BSA raced at home and abroad, including at Brooklands. This French rider on his 1913 TT Model is ready to go. *HMA*

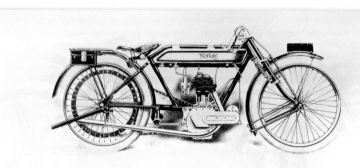

BELOW: This 1912 Triumph
TT Roadster with lightweight
Swan sidecar and disc wheel
covers was the coolest
machine on the road. The rider
looks game for a race. *NPL*

— B. R. S. —

BROOKLANDS ROAD SPECIAL.

2¼ Dunlop Tyres,   79 × 100 = 490 c.c.   B. & B. Carburetter.

PRICE - £60 0 0   With Phillipson Pulley, **£4** extra.

For those who desire exceptional power and speed for competition in a machine suitable for road work.
Each engine undergoes a Brooklands test similar to the B.S. (see opposite page) and is CERTIFIED TO HAVE
EXCEEDED 65 m.p.h. for a lap. It has grand acceleration, is very flexible and, excepting our B.S., is the fastest machine
upon the market. The bearings are in no way "skimped" in order to obtain speed (as so many consider necessary), but
are particularly substantial, as in all our models. Durability is in no way interfered with, the engine being designed to with-
stand the excessive strains due to high speeds. In track parlance, "It will not knock itself to bits."

Model No. 8.—Code Word, "Brookray."

While we have accounts of hot-shoe riders hitting the unpaved roads of America in the 1910s, their experience was dusty and bumpy, and they were hardly able to exploit the increasing speeds available from motorcycles. It's estimated there were fewer than 500 miles of paved road in the entire country in 1910. Bicyclists were the first to lobby for road improvement, and Albert Pope was a major backer of the Good Roads Movement from the 1880s onwards. The first interstate agreement on roads was finally signed in 1914, but while motorcycles and trucks proved incredibly useful at the advent of World War I, the United States remained a backwater between its large cities, with easy rail transport but appalling surface travel. Future president Dwight Eisenhower participated in the first cross-country military expedition in 1919; it took two months to complete (over twice the expected length) and resulted in several deaths en route. He recounted the trip in a 1967 essay, "Through Darkest America with Truck and Tank,"—an accurate, albeit tongue-in-cheek, title.

Four American brands were on sale in the United Kingdom in 1911, but Indian was the only one to send a full racing team abroad. Indian cofounder Oscar Hedstrom sent factory racers for the TT and Brooklands races in 1909 and upped the ante in 1910, bringing himself, several racing bikes, and the world's first professional motorcycle racer, Jake DeRosier. DeRosier was

A flashy hotrod 1914 Zenith Gradua with very early disc wheel covers and perilously dropped handlebars. Perhaps the Klaxon horn is operated using the chin? *TV*

Dunhill's Motorities

Alfred Dunhill inherited his family's saddlery business in 1893 and shifted its attention to the nascent motoring industry in 1895, establishing Duhill's Motorities to supply "everything but the motor." Accessories included horns, lamps, hats, leather riding coats, goggles, picnic sets, watches, and more for men and women, including products made for aviation by the early 1900s. Motorities explicitly catered to motorcycles, advertising in British magazines from their beginnings in 1903. The company's catalog offered over 1,300 ready-made items, although one could order bespoke riding gear, as Elsie Knocker did in 1913 for her very chic green leather riding skirt and coat.

Alfred Dunhill was a committed motorist who loved a fast drive and was so vexed by early speed limits he sold various "bobby dodger" items, including binocular goggles to spot road-side police traps. He also created the signature Tweenie Devil mascot, an imp thumbing his nose at both police and slower motorists, taunting them, "Catch me if you can." Dunhill's riding gear was top-notch, and the company explored new fabrics for waterproofing and wind-cheating over the decades, while focusing increasingly on fine leather accessories and smoking paraphernalia in later years.

Alfred Dunhill Ltd. reconnected with its motoring association in the mid-1990s, hiring motorcycle enthusiasts Nick Ashley and Bill Amberg to design a new line of menswear and leather goods, respectively, to revitalize the brand. Ashley, the son of fashion designer Laura Ashley, is a veteran of the Paris–Dakar race and a dedicated café racer. In 2005, he convinced the Dunhill brass to create the Dunhill Egli-Vincent, a signature motorcycle with details specified by Ashley, including a particular seat hump and kicked-up exhaust. The beasts were painted chocolate brown with gold accents and the Dunhill logo on the side panels, and they were used for publicity, not for public sale. Sadly, the three units made were ultimately decommissioned by removing their logos, and the bikes were sold cheaply, much to Nick Ashley's lament!

a huge star in the United States as a "track man" on the incredibly popular wooden velodromes at the end of the nineteenth century. His mastery of track strategy proved a critical advantage in motorcycle racing, but the 1910 TT was disastrous for Indian, as a rotten batch of inner tubes sent its riders careering into stone walls; brothers Charlie and Harry Collier, on their Matchlesses, won. The next month, however, Indians secured first and third place at a sixty-lap "TT rules" race at Brooklands, and a grudge match was arranged between DeRosier and Charlie Collier. In a two-of-three race, the American's mastery of track craft and drafting made him the winner.

OPPOSITE: Simon "Wizard" O'Donovan (pictured here in 1914) installed engines in his Norton test mule, *Old Miracle*, to gain a speed certificate at Brooklands. *TV*

ABOVE: While Merkel pioneered front and rear springing, this 1914 model has only the rear. This is not the expression of an automobilist—motorcycles are much more fun. *JD*

OPPOSITE: H. Applegate on his 1915 Zenith Gradua with a watercooled Green engine and waterproof suit. Note the black cat mascot—an evergreen trend. *TV*

Taking no chances in 1911, Oscar Hedstrom brought his three best mechanics plus DeRosier to England for TT preparations. The TT organizers had changed the racecourse for 1911 to include Snaefell Mountain, a 1,400-foot climb in 4 miles, in an effort to force British manufacturers to adopt clutches and gears on their single-speed, belt-driven machines. The change meant Indian held an instant advantage, having two speeds, a clutch, and all-chain drive as standard. British makers hurriedly grafted on two- or three-speed rear hubs (the same as a bicycle) for a chance over the big climb. In a show of technical superiority, 1911 was truly an "Indian summer" as Oliver Godfrey rode the first non-English motorcycle to win the TT, followed in by archrival Charlie Collier, riding his Matchless with JAP 90-bore engine—Collier had taken fuel at an unauthorized stop and was disqualified. Charles B. Franklin then moved up to second, and Arthur Moorhouse, the first privateer home, came third. Indian had gained a clean sweep at the toughest race in the world.

Elsie Knocker and Mairi Chisholm

They were the most famous female motorcyclists of the teens and the most famous women of World War I. Elsie Knocker and Mairi Chisholm were dubbed the Angels of Pervyse for their medical triage station set up a mere 100 yards from the Belgian front at Ypres, where they rescued and treated wounded soldiers under the most appalling conditions for the duration of the war. Together they generated more sales of war bonds than any other celebrity, and countless magazine stories profiled these fascinating women, who met through a mutual love of motorcycles.

Knocker, born in 1884, was married with a child by 1906 but soon divorced. To avoid the stigma that came with being a divorcée in socially restrictive Edwardian society, she claimed her husband had been killed in Java, which freed her in the to do as she liked as a "merry widow." She was fascinated by motorcycles and befriended a fast-riding young man whom she entreated to teach her to ride. She became a passionate motorcyclist and owned a string of machines before war broke out in 1914, including a Scott two-stroke, a Douglas flat-twin, and a Chater-Lea with a sidecar. She was a fast and skilled rider who loved a challenge, including competitions on and off-road, and surprised male riders by beating them on difficult terrain. Biographer Diane Atkinson noted of Knocker that "she had an irresistible inclination towards the greatest possible danger"; she loved tearing around the roads of London's outskirts and gained the nickname Gypsy for her membership in the Gypsy Motorcycle Club. She had a custom riding suit in green leather made for her by Alfred Dunhill Ltd., whose early Motorities advertising and catalog catered to exactly such a character: a passionate lover of machines with enough financial wherewithal to purchase or custom order their top-shelf riding gear. Elsie's riding outfit included a skirt with a full-length coat, with double buttons and a belt in the middle to "keep it all together," as she said.

Mairi Lembert Gooden-Chisholm was twelve years younger than Knocker. Her older brother Uailean competed in rallies and speed trials aboard his 425cc Royal Enfield single, and after much entreating, her father bought her a Douglas flat-twin, which she soon learned to both ride and repair. While tearing around the countryside in 1912, she met Elsie Knocker, and both were riding Douglas flat twins—Knocker a Ladies' Model and Mairi a Sports model. Knocker was by then thirty years old, but the pair became inseparable friends and riding companions despite the age difference. They were both competitive and fast riders and loved the challenge of beating other (male) riders in organized trials and on the road. They were very early café racer women.

When war was declared in 1914, Knocker convinced Chisholm to move with her to London and become dispatch riders for the Women's Emergency Corps. Chisholm's riding skills caught the eye of Dr. Hector Munro, who had set up the Flying Ambulance Corps to help neutral Belgium after the German army invaded. Chisholm said Dr. Munro "was deeply impressed with my ability to ride through traffic. He traced me to the Women's Emergency Corps, and said, 'Would you like to go to Flanders?', and I said 'Yes I'd love to!'" The women took their motorcycles with them to the front—Elsie her Chater-Lea, Mairi her Douglas—and their excellent driving skills proved essential during the war; they ferried thousands of wounded men from their "station house" on the front lines to proper field hospitals miles away. They were extensively decorated with medals and honors by the Belgian and British military and were the most celebrated motorcyclists of the war.

OPPOSITE: Shown here in 1913 with her 500cc Douglas Ladies Model, one of her many motorcycles, Elsie Knocker rode in green leather Dunhill riding gear. *NPG*

Tommy Browne, "the Speed Bug," rests atop his Indian single in 1916 with other Indian riders when brand loyalty was at times a matter of fisticuffs. *TV*

Superstar DeRosier had been interviewed in *Motorcycling* magazine in the May 20, 1911, issue just before the TT, and he recounted traveling with his wife in a borrowed Indian sidecar outfit to visit Hatfield, a north London suburb. This was shorthand for the Red Lion pub, situated on the main road connecting London to the north of England, which predated the Ace Café as a café racer hangout by fifty years. While no interview exists documenting DeRosier's thoughts on his fellow hot-shoe riders at the Red Lion, it was a well-known venue for the speedmen (and women) of the day, being far enough out of town to enjoy traffic-free riding through the countryside before development engulfed the area in London's sprawl.

After Indian's stupendous victory in the Isle of Man, the brand offered a TT model in late 1911. This was not a stripped-down racing machine to appeal to the café racer enthusiast but one with the engine capacity stipulated for twin-cylinder motors in the Senior TT: 585cc. Thus, it was eligible for popular "TT rules" races at every track in Britain and was, of course, the first (and only) Indian factory café racer. It's a nearly forgotten model today, and collectors are occasionally vexed by Indians with TT stamped on their crankcases, with the curious displacement of 585cc. No, theirs is not one of the victorious racers come to rest in some Florida barn, but one of the thousands of TT models built after the 1911 victory. Indian did not have it so easy in the 1912–1913 TTs, as other manufacturers got gears too. There was a hiatus in the Isle of Man until 1920 due to World War I, but Indian would continue to enter the TT into the 1920s.

DEMONIAC RIDERS BEFORE THE HOSTILITIES

Amazingly, despite their status as technical pioneers of the motorcycle industry, the French did not love motorcycles in the 1910s, and sightings of bikes on French roads were rare, even in Paris. French commentators before 1914 lamented there was no magazine solely devoted to motorcycles, and *L'Echo des Sports* was the only magazine with a regular motorcycle page. That publication noted in 1911, "There is no question of doubt that the motorcycle in Paris is not popular. A motorcycle would allow a ride every Sunday at very little cost, but it is not 'chic' enough. On his car a man is admired, and that is all he wants!" While the French industry produced some of the fastest racing motorcycles in the world and pioneered racing on public roads as far back as 1895, the motorcycle had fallen out of favor by 1910. This was partly blamed on our speed-mad French kin, the "demoniac" café racer: "At last it is understood—that there is no need to be astride a machine capable of doing sixty miles an hour. Half that speed is sufficient, and comfort has at last replaced the merely speedy—that real madness which induced demoniac people to fly like thunder through the villages, terrifying hens, ducks, children, policemen, and other poultry of that sort." And while the image of policemen as poultry is a fine one, blaming an entire industry's troubles on demoniac riders seems far-fetched. Speed not chic? Never.

Lack of demand did not stop French manufacturers from producing fine machines, and one of them, from Peugeot, was by far the most

Style is everything. This 1920 Harley-Davidson Model J has decorative disc wheel covers and a trendy electric spot lamp in lieu of the heavy factory item. *CG*

ABOVE AND RIGHT: The first
production motorcycle, the 1894
Hildebrand & Wolfmuller, used overhead
valves, but it took the industry a while to
make the idea reliable. This 1914 N.U.T.
has a 1000cc J.A.P. "90 Bore" engine,
an early OHV V-twin with vertical valves,
one of the hottest road/race motors
available in Britain before World War I.
J.A.P. used an effective internal oiling
system relying on internal crankcase
pressure and oil mist. *PT*

OPPOSITE: Pope built the first
production overhead-valve motorcycle
in America from 1912, the 1000cc Model
L, which was the fastest American
roadster when introduced. It took 24
years to see the next American roadster
OHV V-twin, the Crocker. *PT*

advanced motorcycle in the world when revealed in 1913. Peugeot built powerful engines in the 1900s, mostly V-twins, used to great success by Norton and Vindec Special in the first Isle of Man TT. As well, their larger track-racing V-twins, with 2-liter motors powering bikes of a regulation-maximum 110 pounds, dominated the velodromes of Europe. A few of these motors snuck over to the United States, and Indian's Oscar Hedstrom seems to have used one in a 1909 Daytona Beach speed session with an Indian paint scheme. Whether this engine was an Indian-made experiment or simply a test of the French motor is not remembered today.

Peugeot's tour de force was the remarkable 500M of 1913, which was the first double-overhead-camshaft motorcycle in the world. It was also a parallel twin and had four valves per cylinder, making it the precursor to everything fast in the 1980s. This was outer-space technology for 1913, but it was paired with a single-speed belt drive, par for the course in the day. The engine spec was identical to Peugeot's all-conquering four-cylinder auto-racing motor (and was developed by the same engineering team, "the Charlatans"), but the translation to two wheels was not initially successful, and the bike could only reach about 74 miles per hour. That compared quite poorly with other racing bikes of 1913: Charlie Collier's Matchless hit 92 miles per hour, and eight-valve board-track racers from Indian were pushing 100. It wasn't until the early 1920s, with a total redesign using a single overhead camshaft and two valves, that the Peugeot motor was a success. But as a flag planted on French soil for the future of motorcycling, the 500M was astounding.

In Germany, motorcycles had a greater general acceptance, and their industry thrived in the years before 1914. Of the many German makes in production by 1910, however, only NSU had a presence in the United States, in the form of a board-track racer plying the Los Angeles motordrome by 1911. In Britain, NSU and Wanderer were the most common German imports. Curiously, motorcycles were not integrated into Germany's military as they were with British, French, and American forces, but there was one ubiquitous German invention on nearly every 1910s motorcycle: the Bosch magneto. It was a revelation for reliability, replacing the poor batteries of the day, which were typically total-loss dry cells that needed regular replacement and were prone to failure. World War I made the Bosch magneto impossible to secure in Britain and the United States, which spurred other manufacturers, such as Splitdorf and BTH to take up manufacture of this vital instrument. Patent infringement was difficult to enforce when the host countries were at war!

Motorcycling in Europe after 1914 was almost wholly military, and the only speedy motorcyclists were dispatch riders (who replaced horse-mounted couriers) hightailing it across shelled fields, avoiding bomb craters and flying lead. Motorcyclists have always understood the rest of the world holds lethal threats—the road, the car, the dog—but in World War I, they were literal moving targets. Just because you're paranoid doesn't mean they're not trying to kill you! After the madness of the Great War, the European market was flooded with ex-military machines painted in civilian colors, while factories needed a moment to transition away from military production and introduce new models to a public eager to forget the horror. It would take until the 1920s for the technological advances of the internal combustion engine developed for military aircraft to be integrated into the motorcycle sphere, first by clever home tuners and then by manufacturers looking for more power with reliability. The OHV motor would come to the fore in Europe in the 1920s, thanks to the urgency of making aircraft reliable in the war.

OPPOSITE TOP: This 1914 Sunbeam was modified by Harold Haring using an overhead-valve cylinder head from a WWI plane back when special builders led the industry. *HMA*

OPPOSITE BOTTOM: American riding fashion circa 1918 consisted of heavy woolen riding sweaters, neckties, berets, flat caps, jodhpurs, and lace-up logger boots. *CG*

BELOW: A dashing gent on his hot rod 1918 Rudge Multi poses in seaside woolens, with tie and pocket square, as his wife and children look on. *HMA*

2

IIA - 7113

THE 1920s: THE ROAR OF THE TWENTIES

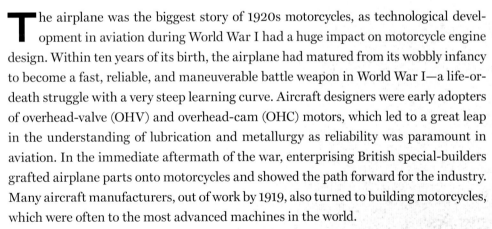

The airplane was the biggest story of 1920s motorcycles, as technological development in aviation during World War I had a huge impact on motorcycle engine design. Within ten years of its birth, the airplane had matured from its wobbly infancy to become a fast, reliable, and maneuverable battle weapon in World War I—a life-or-death struggle with a very steep learning curve. Aircraft designers were early adopters of overhead-valve (OHV) and overhead-cam (OHC) motors, which led to a great leap in the understanding of lubrication and metallurgy as reliability was paramount in aviation. In the immediate aftermath of the war, enterprising British special-builders grafted airplane parts onto motorcycles and showed the path forward for the industry. Many aircraft manufacturers, out of work by 1919, also turned to building motorcycles, which were often to the most advanced machines in the world.

By the teens, motorcycles had become fast and reliable, but each country experienced a tipping point when cars outnumbered motorcycles on the road, and bikes evolved into pleasure objects (or even luxuries) rather than necessary transport. That change happened earliest in the United States, thanks to Henry Ford's Model T. Initially the T cost an exorbitant $850 in 1909, but by the early 1920s it had fallen to $290—little more than the price of a new Harley-Davidson and much

OPPOSITE: Despite their unusual five-cylinder engine in the front wheel, Megolas were very competitive. This snappily dressed German rider sits on his 1921 Sport model. *HMA*

ABOVE: In the mid-1920s, California riders began modifying their Harley-Davidsons as cut downs for speed and style. The middle bike has been converted to a single-cylinder in an early example of a chopped frame. *RO*

OPPOSITE: All the gear, all the time. This 1920s rider models the latest all-leather protective fashion, complete with cinched-waist jacket, jodhpurs, flying helmet, and goggles. *TV*

less than a Henderson four-cylinder ($435). But motorcycles were (and remain) far more exciting, and the liberation of bikes from utilitarian duties meant riders could enjoy motorcycles for their own sake. Of course, they had *always* been fun, but with the liberation of motorcycles from work, fewer excuses were necessary.

In prosperous England and the United States, and eventually the rest of Europe, the late teens became the Roaring Twenties, which echoed with the blast of powerful engines from increasingly reliable motorcycles and cars. While lightweight bikes dominated European roads and much of the English market, they nearly disappeared in America, which grew its own heavy-duty branch of the motorcycle tree. The Art Deco movement changed the look of bikes in the 1920s, with general prosperity reflected in shiny nickel plating. The angular shape of pressed-metal mudguards and tanks gave way to "styled" parts, gaining graceful decorative curves. Art Deco also transformed the visual representation of motorcycles in advertising, as graphic artists competed to out-style each other in presenting two-wheelers as geometric, hurtling masses, in imitation of Jacques-Henri Lartigue's photographic distortions of racing cars (created by using a slow horizontal shutter and a panning camera motion).

Such imagery changed how motorcycles inhabited people's thoughts, planting visual clues that bikes were chic accessories for the well heeled or those aspiring to be. As the 1920s progressed, the development of German

Bauhaus design integrated both the futurist and Art Deco languages, codifying the "modern look" of clean lines and simplified production. The spare and balanced geometry of Bauhaus, its love of color blocks and collaged photos and paper, led to a golden age of motorcycle brochures and posters. Probably the best example is closest to the source: BMW, whose very logo could have been lifted from a Bauhaus instruction book and whose bikes rapidly evolved from their first rather pokey models in 1923 to the sleek, fast, and elegant machines of the late 1920s, as the factory became a devotee to the cult of speed to a degree unmatched in the industry.

The inexpensive car freed the two-wheeled vehicle to do what it does best: deliver an erotic injection of life, providing thrills, excitement, prestige, and danger in equal measure. Very few automobiles of the period, no matter how sexy, delivered the all-senses stimulation of a motorbike, as all but the most sporting automobiles insulated the driver from the assaults of nature and the road. The motorcyclist, then as now, embraces all these as the essential appeal of a vulnerable, sensate existence.

As the number of cars far surpassed the number of motorcycles, the increase in traffic paved the way to improved roads, which benefitted motorcyclists greatly. Soon that fresh pavement wore the long black streaks left by the increasingly fast bikes of the 1920s.

OPPOSITE: Racer on the road! George Tucker won the Isle of Man TT and this race at Brooklands on his Norton 16H and racing sidecar in 1924. *TV*

ABOVE: "Welsh Wizard" Charles Sgonina kept his racers road registered, like his 1921 machine with a homemade overhead-camshaft engine in a Sunbeam Sprint chassis. *HMA*

Even small two-strokes were sprinted and entered in trials in the 1920s, as with this brand new, fully-equipped sub-250cc machine with dropped 'bars at a road trial. *TV*

THE AMERICAN SCENE

The American motorcycle industry had been leveled by World War I, as inflation hit the price of both labor and materials. By the mid-1920s, what had been a thriving marketplace with hundreds of small manufacturers had been narrowed to just a few major players: Harley-Davidson, Indian, Excelsior-Henderson, Ace, Cleveland and Ner-A-Car. Of these, Ace built the fastest road machines, as William Henderson (who'd sold his original four-cylinder company to Schwinn/Excelsior in 1917) brought his design genius to bear. The Ace Four was the fastest production motorcycle in the world until the Brough Superior SS100 arrived in 1924, but Ace lost money on every machine sold, and not many riders got to experience its pleasures—until the design was sold to Indian in 1927.

With a track record of selling bikes abroad, and a few million Americans having seen Europe during the war, Indian, Harley-Davidson, and Excelsior placed increasing attention on international markets at the start of the 1920s. Both H-D and Indian built special road racers for Britain, Europe, Australia, and Japan in configurations never offered at home: special overhead-valve and even overhead-camshaft racers with fenders and a front brake. European race rules demanded two brakes, so years before American bikes got decent brakes at home, they had them on foreign tracks. American riders drooled at tantalizing photos of a Harley-Davidson eight-valve V-twin with a three-speed gearbox and drum brakes, or the Indian A45 750cc OHV V-twins (one of which hit 129 miles per hour at El Mirage in 1926) with street equipment.

The two manufacturers entered the lightweight market with European-style bikes in the early 1920s, both flat-twins and small singles. Indian purchased an OHC Velocette Model K in 1925 to study (and copy); it became the Prince model, available with a side-valve, OHV, or OHC engine. Indian again sent special racers to the Isle of Man TT starting in 1920 and developed Grand Prix racers for Europe, including an OHC racing version of the Prince that appeared at the Montlhéry speedbowl in 1926. That was the last time an American manufacturer would compete on

a Grand Prix circuit until the 1960s, as a tariff war with Britain and Europe in 1926 increased the price of American motorcycles by 30 percent or more, decimating sales abroad. The motivation to develop special racers for Europe evaporated along with the sales, as did exploration of "British-style" light-weight machines such as the H-D Peashooter and Indian Prince. American companies turned inward, focusing on competition within their borders, which created a distinct motorcycle evolution toward big, heavy side-valve V-twins that forever after defined the American motorcycle style.

In the mid-1920s, American riders developed a distinct branch of café racer style: the cut down. While best known as the original American cus-tom, the cut down style was clearly a "racer on the road." These machines were typically Harley-Davidsons with their front fenders removed, rear fenders shortened (or "bobbed"), and handlebars kept low and wide, which suited dirt roads. Cut downs were stripped for speed, with performance gains coming from weight loss, until the twin-cam Harley-Davidson JDH appeared in 1928. The JDH cut down became the original ton-up special,

Adalberto Garelli designed fast two-stroke 350cc split singles like this 1922 Raid model that started the racing careers of of Tazio Nuvolari and Achille Varzi. *HMA*

ABOVE: The 1923 Norton 16H Sports was a gentleman's mount, and this fellow has his summer outfit sorted—lightweight leather jerkin, gloves, and always a necktie. *PdO*

OPPOSITE: The 1924 Norton Model 18 was their first super-sports overhead valve model, shown here with dramatically dropped 'bars and a useless toffee-tin front brake. The white-out cleaned up the photo for magazines and catalogs. *HMA*

easily tuned for over 100 miles per hour, and the speed equal of any motorcycle in the world. One popular modification was the use of a small spot lamp in place of heavy headlamps, giving the bikes a very compact and modern appearance. The cut down style was widely copied and is the rootstock of the American custom motorcycle. It also fits into the legacy of café racer style, although the racers it emulated—board trackers and hillclimbers—looked different from European Grand Prix machines, especially as racing became a strictly domestic affair in the USA.

At the end of the 1920s, the cut down developed further, as builders altered the frames of their machines to lower the saddle height and shorten the wheelbase. This resulted in a lower center of gravity and better handling and lent a modern look to older bikes. Factory design studios at H-D and Indian took note of these machines, and by the early 1930s they began to adapt the cut down style for production models. Like most café racer trends, the donor motorcycles tended to be inexpensive older machines, modified for speed. A Harley-Davidson JDH Cut Down was the ultimate American hot-rod until the Crocker Big Twin appeared in 1936, and today a real 1920s cut down is a treasured rarity, as they're recognized as world-class early café racers.

THE RISE OF THE BRITISH HYBRID

The British motorcycle scene rebounded quickly in the 1920s, as riders were eager to get on with living after so much wartime dying. The roar of the '20s seemed a combination of a ringing in the ear for those too close to artillery fire, the din of a party in full swing, and the sound of an engine "on song" with the throttle opened wide. Lessons learned in aviation about the internal combustion engine were integrated into motorcycle design, initially from riders with access to aircraft parts, who built hot-rod specials at home. While OHV and OHC motors had been seen on motorcycles before World War I, they were unreliable due to inadequate lubrication and poor metallurgy; their use in aircraft solved many of these issues. Post-war, intrepid speedmen such as George Dance grafted OHV aircraft cylinders onto their motorcycle engines for more power. Dance used the 1913 Sunbeam engine as the basis for his experiments, and by 1919 his hybrid Sunbeams were an unbeatable sprint racers. They were gorgeously light and slender, having been pared down to their essence—they had no fenders or oil tank, a simple leather-covered metal saddle, and no front brake at all. The gorgeous style of Dance's specials influenced stylists of the 1920s, as a kind of ideal machine that was also the fastest thing on wheels.

Impatience

Yonnie Selma was the original "girl on a motorcycle," although all but the most dedicated film historians promptly forgot her. It took a visionary artist to place a nude woman on a speeding bike in 1928 (even the futurists missed that trick), making Charles Dekeukeleire's *Impatience* the first film to eroticize the motorcycle. Films of the silent era had often featured motorcycles to add kinetic energy to a story, but none had made an explicit connection between a swiftly moving, vibrating motorcycle and a woman's body. Dekeukeleire was a Belgian artist working within the great artistic movements of the era—futurism, dada, and cubism. *Impatience* was intended as a pure cinematic experience without a narrative and has four characters: the motorcycle, the woman, the mountain, and abstract shapes. With no story, it makes visual poetry of a speeding motorcycle for its own sake, and it did so for the first time in cinema. The impact of this rarely seen film can only be guessed at; did Jack Cardiff know of it before directing *The Girl on a Motorcycle* in 1968? The parallels are striking, and some scenes nearly identical. No matter the truth, *Impatience* clearly set the pattern for sexualizing the fast motorcycle, and relating the machine to a woman's body, with the possibility of an erotic bond between them.

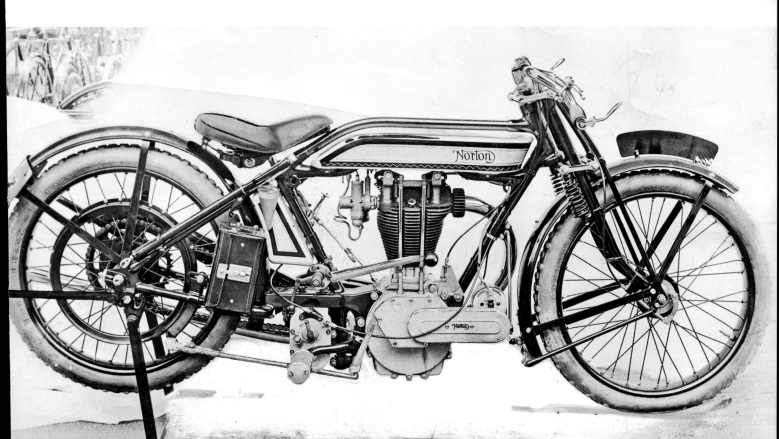

OPPOSITE: Charlie Sgonina's café racer in its ultimate 1923 iteration, with bevel-driven double-overhead-camshaft engine dominating its delicate Sunbeam Sprint chassis. *PdO*

TOP: Harley-Davidson JD riders in California's Central Valley display a variety of speed modifications in the mid-1920s, with front fenders cut or removed and headlamps replaced by lighter spot lamps, on their way to establishing the cut down style. Their homogenous riding attire is notable. *TV*

ABOVE: A very special American 1924 Excelsior with Triumph Ricardo 4-valve cylinder heads (which made for a powerful 8-valve roadster) grafted on by R. Taymans of Brussels. *TV*

D. Lewis

One of the world's oldest motorcycle-clothing manufacturers, Lewis Leathers, traces its origins to 1896, when David Isaacs opened D. Lewis Ltd. at 124 Great Portland Street, London. A canny seventy-four-year lease ensured the business remained in situ right through the classic rocker years and into the 1980s.

D. Lewis started humbly, reselling and repairing clothes and making menswear as one of the earliest clothing manufacturers in London. By 1922, the firm had incorporated and was at the center of a booming business selling specialized gear to aviators, motorists, and motorcyclists. Its flying suits and protective jackets and trousers—made of cotton, leather, or wool—were both stylish and functional. Leather flying jackets, designed for open-cockpit planes in World War I, were quickly adapted for motorcyclists, and as racing rules demanded protective clothing in the 1920s racing, distinctive leather gear was developed for riders on two wheels. Double-breasted jackets and leather trousers held up with suspenders were de rigueur on tracks right through World War II, but the introduction of the Lightning zipper in the 1920s gave rise to a streamlined style the motorcyclists quickly adopted.

The D. Lewis No. 702 jacket of the late 1920s would be recognizable to any motorcyclist today, with its angled-zipper front and wide notched lapels, perfect for folding over to protect a rider's neck from the wind. It also had the original D-shaped pocket up front, inherited from aviation gear, which leather cognoscenti recognize as proper vintage motorcycle gear. The form of the No. 702 was seen around the world later in the 1930s, and many other manufacturers claimed this original "biker jacket" design as their own, but to all evidence, it was D. Lewis who first commercially produced the style and advertised it in its catalogs. After World War II, the style would become known universally as the biker jacket, especially after its star turn as a secondary character in *The Wild One* in 1953.

OPPOSITE: The 1926 Brough Superior SS100 was the king of the road, and riders around the world ordered their own bespoke examples, from India and Australia to Europe, as with this German rider, H. Wohanka. *HMA*

Other clever engineer-tuners adapting aircraft ideas included Harold Haring, who built an OHV Sunbeam just like Dance's in 1920; and the "Welsh Wizard," Charles Sgonina, a demon rider on road and track and a member of the Triumph and Norton TT racing teams before World War I. In 1920, Sgonina modified his Norton 16H racer with an OHV top end, which gave a noticeable increase in performance. Sgonina continuously developed his special machine, which was always road-registered, as a proper 1920s café racer. He next built a chain-drive OHC conversion using a specially cast timing-side crankcase. While it proved fast, its long chain was frightening, whipping at high revs. He split the chain run, using the magneto as a middle sprocket, but the chain-drive OHC motor would not

Douglas
'Leader of the Pack'

Douglas.

1928
494 cc. I.O.M. T.T. MODEL.
£88

be successful until Weller designed the slipper chain tensioner, which AJS licensed in 1927 for its OHC roadsters and racers. In 1923, Sgonina totally redesigned his engine with a shaft-and-bevel-driven double-OHC motor, installed in a Sunbeam Sprint frame. The resulting machine was an elegant beast and the apex café racer of the early 1920s.

George Brough emerged in 1919 as the ultimate builder of fast road machines. He'd proven his mettle competing on his father's eponymous motorcycles from the age of sixteen and was a crack rider with tremendous panache and a winning personality—everyone loved George. He was the ultimate fan of racers on the road and built the hottest street bikes in the world from 1919 onwards, as Brough Superiors. He insisted on racing engines for his road bikes, as he was primarily interested in building the fastest road-going motorcycles in the world. He succeeded right through the late 1930s, when the Crocker Big Twin and Vincent HRD Series A Rapide stole his crown in 1936. Brough was the first true master of motorcycle advertising copy, being a born sloganeer and congenial

ABOVE: The 1928 Douglas Isle of Man TT Model was a special super sports machine with a wet sump motor and engine development by the legendary Freddie Dixon. *TV*

OPPOSITE: Only a wealthy German family could afford BMW's first overhead-valve racer for the road, the 1926 R37, and this young lady could handle the speed. *HMA*

ABOVE: "Joe" and "Nello" with a pair of super hot customized 1926 Harley-Davidson JDs, early Cut Downs with dropped 'bars, bobbed fenders, and small spotlamps. *TV*

OPPOSITE: Scott motorcycles used a triangulated frame with terrific handling, and their water-cooled two-stroke twin-cylinder engine was quick and torquey, a mix that made for lively performance and an unforgettable yowl at open throttle. *PT*

braggart. He built a spindly, ultralight sprinter around a supertuned JAP side-valve engine, with a slim nickel-plated saddle tank and extra bracing for the frame. He gave it a nickname—Spit and Polish—and it proved the first British side-valve V-twin that could top 100 miles per hour; Brough secured plenty of orders for its production version, the SS80 of 1922. A mere two years later, JAP introduced a new 1,000cc OHV V-twin racing motor, the KTOR, with inclined valves and a hemispherical combustion chamber. George Brough built a motorcycle around it, the SS100, which was the first production road-ster in the world guaranteed for 100 miles per hour, an astounding speed at the time. The SS100 was also the most expensive motorcycle in the world; you could buy a decent house in a London suburb for its £180 price tag. And the maximum speed limit in England was still 20 miles per hour!

Freddie Barnes lacked the personal extravagance of George Brough, but his Zeniths earned their riders more Gold Stars at Brooklands, for laps of 100 miles per hour or more during a race. Zenith built supertuned sin-gles and twins in the 1920s, with engines by JAP (the KTOR, just like the SS100) as well as Martlett, Blackburne, Motosacoche, and Anzani (in two-valve and ferocious four-valve configurations). Buying a supersports Zenith meant individual attention from Barnes, a veteran racer and tuner, who could offer a rider the ultimate in road performance. Your author owned the Zenith Championship model displayed at the 1925 Olympia show; with its 1,000cc JAP KTOR racing engine it was every bit as fast as an SS100, albeit less a luxury machine than a flat-out hot rod. Mine had presumably been road-ridden and raced before ending up in Argentina, where it recorded 116 miles per hour to take the South American speed

record. It gained a supercharger in 1930 and was enlarged to 1,600cc and renamed Super Kim by Roberto Sigrand, a demon racer and very brave fellow, who rode this beast at 130 miles per hour on a dirt road.

The 1920s were the golden age for awesome OHV V-twins from Zenith, Brough Superior, McEvoy, Coventry-Eagle, and Montgomery, among others. They were often attached to an ultralight sporting sidecar, with a steam-bent ash chassis and a thin aluminum skin, shaped like boats or zeppelins. Sporting sidecars of the 1920s weighed less than 100 pounds, being a simple tube frame and skimpy body with buggy springs, which did little to impede the rapid progress of a motorcycle and gave a reasonably comfortable if thrilling ride for a passenger. Sidecar makers Mills-Fulford, Watsonian, Swallow (which evolved into Jaguar cars), and dozens of others set up shop in this three-wheeled boom time. The sports/racing sidecar was a defining feature of the 1920s, decked out in two-tone paint, polished aluminum, and disc wheel coverings, sometimes for all three wheels. Such outfits were very light, fast, and stylish beyond compare, the ultimate Jazz Age transportation. In many ways, their like has never been seen since, and the café racer scene never truly embraced the fast sidecar again.

A 1925 Brough Superior SS100 was king of the road then and is still a fast machine. This one was ridden across the United States by the author, seen here crossing the Rockies at Glacier National Park, during the 2018 Motorcycle Cannonball cross-country rally. *PDO*

T. E. Lawrence "of Arabia": The Shakespeare of Speed

Thomas Edward Lawrence was the most famous motorcyclist of the early twentieth century. He was also, as Nick Clements writes in *Men's File*, a "subculture of one": an individual so particular he's an uneasy fit in any group. But he definitely overlapped with café racers, being a man devoted of to the gods of speed, who would only ride the fastest motorcycle on earth: the Brough Superior SS100. He owned six of them in succession and wrote eloquently on the joys of flat-out riding over an empty countryside. His letters were used in Brough Superior catalog testimonials because they were sheer poetry: "I could write you pages on the lustfulness of moving swiftly."

His writing in *The Mint,* published posthumously in 1936, beautifully depicts the peculiar effects of fast riding on one's senses. His essay "The Road," recounting an afternoon's ride through the English countryside, is a masterpiece of storytelling:

"The extravagance in which my surplus emotion expressed itself lay on the road. So long as roads were tarred blue and straight; not hedged; and empty and dry, so long I was rich . . .

Boanerges is a top-gear machine, as sweet in that as most single-cylinders in middle. I chug lordly past the guard-room and through the speed limit at no more than sixteen. Round the bend, past the farm, and the way straightens. Now for it. The engine's final development is fifty-two horse-power. A miracle that all this docile strength waits behind one tiny lever for the pleasure of my hand. Another bend: and I have the honour of one of England's straightest and fastest roads. The burble of my exhaust unwound like a long cord behind me. Soon my speed snapped it, and I heard only the cry of the wind which my battering head split and fended aside. The cry rose with my speed to a shriek: while the air's coldness streamed like two jets of iced water into my dissolving eyes. I screwed them to slits, and focused my sight two hundred yards ahead of me on the empty mosaic of the tar's gravelled undulations . . .

Like arrows the tiny flies pricked my cheeks: and sometimes a heavier body, some house-fly or beetle, would crash into face or lips like a spent bullet. A glance at the speedometer: seventy-eight. Boanerges is warming up. I pull the throttle right open, on the top of the slope, and we swoop flying across the dip, and up-down up-down the switchback beyond: the weighty machine launching itself like a projectile with a whirr of wheels into the air at the take-off of each rise, to land lurchingly with such a snatch of the driving chain as jerks my spine like a rictus. . .

He ambles at forty-five and when roaring his utmost, surpasses the hundred. A skittish motor-bike with a touch of blood in it is better than all the riding animals on earth, because of its logical extension of our faculties, and the hint, the provocation, to excess conferred by its honeyed untiring smoothness. Because Boa loves me, he gives me five more miles of speed than a stranger would get from him.

Lawrence was killed on his sixth Brough Superior, George VI, in 1935, while traveling at high speed in hilly country near his home, Clouds Hill. Coming over a hill, he swerved to avoid a pair of boys on bicycles and hit a ditch, a hedge, and his head, which put an end to a brilliant mind. Winston Churchill wept openly at his funeral, lamenting, "We shall not see his like again."

POSTWAR EUROPE

The Treaty of Versailles hastened the development of motorcycles in Germany, as aircraft manufacture was banned. BMW was a prime example, turning to motorcycle building from 1923. While its first machine was the side-valve R32, the company emerged as a full-blooded sports manufacturer in 1925 with the R37, an OHV flat-twin with double the power of the R32. Many other famous German makes made their debut during the boom period of the 1920s, including DKW, Horex, Neander, Standard, Windhoff, and Zündapp. Germans took to motorcycles in a big way in the Weimar era with motorcycle registrations far outnumbering automobiles all the way through the late 1950s—the opposite of trends in the United States. By 1929, Germany had overtaken England as the world's biggest producer of motorcycles, with 195,000 units built (versus 164,000). Naturally, the subculture of fast motorcycles thrived there in the 1920s and 1930s, with stunning examples of racers on the road. While BMW designed its own engines, other manufacturers used motors from JAP, Motosacoche, and Küchen for their sports machines, preferring to differentiate themselves with unique chassis designs.

Included among such designs is the work of Ernst Neumann-Neander, who first built aluminum-beam-framed racers in the early 1920s. Production Neander motorcycles used steel frames with cadmium plating, bulbous fuel tanks, rocking forks, and a shockingly modern saddle design, giving them a timeless look. The Neander with JAP sports V-twin motor was an amazingly competent machine, and remarkably stylish too, looking like a 1920s sci-fi future.

Other chassis experiments of the 1920s included the work, in France, of Georges Roy, with his hub-center-steered Majestics; and, of more interest to café racer fans, Marcel Guiguet, whose MGC used a totally cast-aluminum chassis that integrated both the fuel and oil tanks. The MGC was a visionary machine, a hot sportbike with an amazingly futuristic look, that predated the adoption of aluminum as a chassis material by half a century. Being so avant-garde had its disadvantages, as aluminum casting had not truly matured, and his hollow chassis tended to both leak from porous castings and crack under hard use. But they were amazing and beautiful machines in gleaming polished aluminum.

T. E. Lawrence was the most famous motorcyclist after WWI and rode Brough Superior SS100s to satisfy his love of speed, about which he wrote eloquently. *BS*

In Italy, Moto Guzzi was founded in 1921, building flat single-cylinder bikes with integrated three-speed gearboxes and a modern chassis. Early production models used F-head cylinders but had good sporting performance, as they were very light and low. Their OHC four-valve C4V of 1924 won the European Championship; examples were occasionally seen on the road as far from home as Brazil and Argentina, and the model founded a lineage of increasingly exotic racers that peaked in 1956 with Moto Guzzi's incredible V-8. In the 1920s, British motorcycles were revered in Italy, and future four-wheeled Grand Prix stars, including Tazio Nuvolari and Achille Varzi, raced Sunbeams and Nortons at the start of their careers. However, the home product soon gained prominence on Italian roads, with Frera, Bianchi, Gilera, and Benelli making up the *pentarchia*, or five major manufacturers of Italy. The Italians, more than any other culture, were mad for speed, and their manufacturers emphasized competition and racers on the road to an unparalleled degree. Their amazing speed-focused designs would flourish from the 1950s onwards, when they firmly staked their claim as the world's number-one builders of factory café racers.

A single-port 1928 Sunbeam TT90 road racer with optional Brooklands tank and short Dodson saddle was a vintage motorcycle with thrilling performance. *PdO*

THE 1930s: PROMENADE PERCY AND THE BOB JOB

The 1930s were a time of tremendous social upheaval, a decade born amid financial crisis and ending on the precipice of global conflict. The decade brought tremendous changes to motorcycling, as factories disappeared or changed ownership while the survivors built in reliability by adding weight to their machines. The American industry shrank to just two manufacturers, although Britain retained a diversity of brands, albeit held mostly under conglomerates. Mainland European factories went through similar difficulties but took the lead in the industry in technological development. Supercharged multicylinder race machines saw their fullest expressions in Grand Prix racing in the mid-1930s, with BMW and Gilera taking world speed records and DKW, Moto Guzzi, and BMW taking TT wins. Such exotic technology would not come under the café racer umbrella until the 1970s, but riders were still spoiled for choice in the 1930s, with genuine 100-mile-per-hour roadsters becoming more common from almost every major manufacturer as the decade progressed. As a cultural phenomenon, riders of café racers were mentioned in the letters section of every motorcycle magazine in every language, although it was in England that they were finally identified by name.

OPPOSITE: Long after the Collier brothers quit racing, they carried on building high-quality singles and V-twins with a sporting flair, like this 1930 Model X/2, a modern, fast mount ideal for a Promenade Percy in plus-fours. *HMA*

THE PROMENADE PERCY

The term "seaside promenade Percy" first appeared in the letters section of motorcycle magazines in the early 1930s to describe fans of café racers. The promenade in question was Southend-on-Sea, 30 miles east of London, which was a popular hangout for young riders, who made a spectacle of themselves with their dandyish gear, polished-up bikes, and engine revving. Southend has a 7-mile-long beach, the Talza Arcade, and the Kursaal amusement park and music venue as well as second-longest pleasure pier in the world (1.34 miles long). It was an excellent riding destination and a pleasant spot to meet other riders and tourist girls. By 1932 the term was shortened in the press to "Promenade Percy," which (accurately) alters the implication that the seaside is not required for these Percys: it is the Percys themselves who promenade, as in take a leisurely walk or ride. Perfect. We can assume Percy refers to Percy Bysshe Shelley, the Romantic poet and libertine, who died young and beautiful at age thirty in 1822. There's a demasculinizing taunt in the term, as Percy was hardly the by-the-rules racing he-man of Norton factory racer Jimmy Simpson, who is referred to in the letters at the apex male motorcyclist. The same could be said of the term café racer when it was coined in the 1950s for an identical motorcycling subculture: "real men" risked their necks on racetracks, while café racers merely played at racing and considered chasing girls more important than chasing glory. It's a taunt aimed at youth cultures the world over.

A pair of fast 1930 Standard AS500s with Swiss MAG engines, dropped 'bars, and straight pipes at a café break in Thuringia, Germany. *HMA*

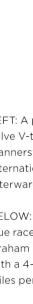

LEFT: A pair of Husqvarna overhead-valve V-twins designed by Folke Mannerstedt, built for the 1929 International Six Days Trials, and afterwards developed for racing. *HMA*

BELOW: The Rudge Ulster was a true race replica in 1929, celebrating Graham Walker's 1928 Ulster GP win, with a 4-valve motor capable of 100 miles per hour in the right hands. *TV*

BOTTOM: Oh, the places we'll go! Young riders with family money get the hottest bikes, always. This pair in 1930 Sao Paulo ride a full-race Moto Guzzi C4V and a Rudge Sports on Brazil's dirt roads. *TV*

From the *Western Gazette* of February 12, 1932: "Pukka riders must not be confused with those 'bright Percys', the promenade pests, who floated up and down their main streets and sea fronts adorned in spotless suits with carefully oiled hair, looking for some fair damsel to adorn their pillion seat." The *The Motor Cycle* columnist known as Nitor joined the chorus of condemnation, lamenting in 1934: "The first of the summer letters on the genus *Seaside Promenade Percy* has appeared in the local paper—a Hastings one. In the Island at TT time I saw quite a few examples, or perhaps heard is the correct word, for the trouble with the species is its infantile delight in screaming off the mark, and making as much noise and nuisance as is possible." Arthur L. Frost paints a colorful picture of the scene in *The Motor Cycle* on October 24, 1934: "The Mutual Admiration MCC has headquarters which appear to be somewhere on the Southend promenade. These gentlemen do not waste petrol or wear out their machines by entering trials or touring long distances, but sit on them stationary in a group and endeavor to persuade promenading fairies to sample their pillions. Once successful, they depart, complete with full elbow movement, making good use of the accelerator of their nice noisy sports models, while their remaining pals cast admiring glances. The club appears to be very go-ahead, as meetings are held

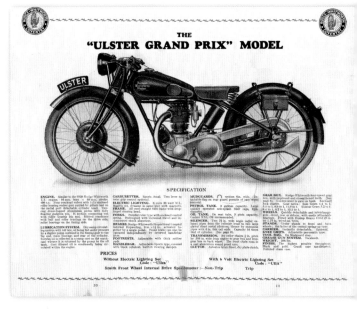

every night, weather permitting, and on Sundays the members hardly leave headquarters, except when they're engaged in 'Simpsoning' up and down the seafront with their pillions bedecked in beach pyjamas."

But of course, such riders congregated in many places: London, too, had its Promenade Percys, according to "250 Velo" (August 16, 1934): "I live in London . . . they are not content to 'Simpson' up or down the main road once, but do so perhaps half a dozen times during their evening run. Then there are the he-men who take off their fishtail extensions, and, replacing them with copper piping, tear up the road to show the boys that they can make changes 'like the racer we saw at so-and-so'. Or what nice thirds they have in their four-speed boxes. They will grow out of it in time." Another: "They are usually elaborately dressed, and possess modern, fast mounts. Their object in obtaining such motorcycles is difficult to understand." Which only proves the writer's lack of imagination. Oh, how the average rider would secretly love to don a high-collar leather Stormgard, turn his flat cap backwards, and ride his Norton International to the seaside and pick up sea-salty tourist girls!

MODERN, FAST MOUNTS

"Modern, fast mounts" in 1930s England included an incredible range of machines, mostly in the classic British single-cylinder style, although a very fast V-twin was still an option for the well heeled. A fast rider was spoiled for choice, and as the decade progressed, design trends led to flashier styling—rounded chrome tanks and elegant fender lines with contemporary

OPPOSITE: Ernst Neumann's design masterpiece, the Neander, was licensed to Opel in 1930 and sold as the Motoclub. They handled beautifully and were coveted by fast riders. *TV*

ABOVE: Carlos Corsi had a Moto Guzzi dealership in Buenos Aires in 1929 and raced this overhead-camshaft 500SS model. In 1932 he rode it to Uspallata pass (elevation 12,572 feet), where the *Cristo Redentor de los Andes* statue was erected in 1904. *JVM*

LEFT: A gang of Bavarian riders in 1930 sport a variety of riding gear, from woolens and berets to full leather and flying caps. Neckties were de rigeur through the 1940s. *TV*

Phil Irving

Australian engineer Phil Irving, on right in photo, is best known for designing Vincent's V-twins, the world's fastest production road bikes from their debut in 1936 until Kawasaki brought out the 750cc H2 in 1972. While still a student in Melbourne in the 1920s, Irving fit the description of a Promenade Percy, riding a flashy, highly tuned AJS Big Port racer on the road and favoring very smart riding outfits. In his excellent 1992 autobiography, he complains about the delay of his suitcase on arriving in London in 1930 leaving him without a decent tuxedo: "There's little doubt in my mind that 'clothes maketh the man'." Photos from Australian club runs prove his enthusiasm for the latest styles: berets, white knit college sweaters and jodhpurs—on a bike with total-loss oiling, designed to fling its dirty oil to the road—and invariably, a collared shirt with a necktie.

Irving's stylish taste extended to his motorcycles. In 1925, he built an AJS café racer with an outrageous paint job and a motor tuned up with factory racing parts. "Coloured tanks were starting to become fashionable, but I decided to strike a new note by getting my tank copper-plated, and then lacquered by a special process which made the copper resemble nine-carat gold," he wrote. "With two black panels and AJS transfers on the sides, the tank looked very fine . . . I made a pair of almost straight handlebars only 25" wide, which was very narrow at the period, but was a

length revived ten years later, on the Vincent-HRD. The mudguards were [painted] with a new crackle-finish enamel . . . I must say it looked magnificent and handled beautifully with the narrow 'bars. At one lunchtime I left it glinting in the sun in the part of Collins Street [Victoria] known as 'the Block' . . . and on returning had to push through a ring of onlookers intrigued by the unusual colour scheme and business-like appearance of the bike."

While not remembered as a motorcycle hooligan, Irving's AJS suggests otherwise; it was very flashy and devoid of a muffler! In the manner of the twenty-first-century café racers to come, it also featured flat bars and no fenders, which proved uncomfortable in the rain. But the bike was a blast: "I set off solo with a tank full of Driscol [racing fuel], an open exhaust pipe, no front mudguard and false numbers [plates swapped from another machine], along the unsealed winding Princes Highway for a truly memorable ride. There was very little traffic, and with about 24 horsepower propelling a 190-pound machine, the performance was exhilarating in the extreme. Luckily, no policemen spoilt the fun . . ." Even a motorcycle-industry icon was not above bending the law in pursuit of speed in high style. Irving's charmingly readable columns for *The Motorcycle* have been collected in such books as *Tuning for Speed,* earning him an enduring reputation as the speedman's best friend.

Art Deco flair. King of the road for most of the 1930s was still the Brough Superior SS100, the only machine guaranteed to top 100 miles per hour. But some needed more speed. C. R. Hobbs commissioned the factory to build Moby Dick, a '29 SS100 with 1,200cc displacement, hot cams, and twin carbs, which was probably the fastest road bike in the world in 1930. An individual using the pen name of Castor in *Motorcycling* tested it, reaching 106 miles per hour in second gear, and estimating it to be good for 120, but on what road would that have been possible in 1931? Even Land Speed Racers could only find three: at Arpajon near Montlhéry; in Gyón, Hungary; and the Carrigrohane Straight outside Cork, Ireland. Moby Dick wasn't a speed-record bike—it was "just" a café racer—so its top speed was never officially measured.

Among the motorcycles built for mere mortals, Ariel's Red Hunter was a perfect example of a "modern, fast mount." For 1934, Edward Turner magically transformed the mundane Model F into a fabulously chic, high-performance all-rounder, via a judicious application of chrome, glossy red paint, and graceful lines. Turner next revamped Triumph's single-cylinder models with pretty chrome gas tanks, metallic silver paint with blue pinstripes, and a kick to the fender lines, creating the magnificent Tiger 80 and 90 models. For 1938 he designed a compact parallel twin engine that fit into the Tiger 90 chassis and called it the Speed Twin, which sent ripples of excitement around the world, as it combined scintillating multicylinder

After countless Brooklands and TT wins, Sunbeam's last production racer was the 1933 Model 95, which was also available as a road bike, with this fantastic pie-plate speedometer. *HMA*

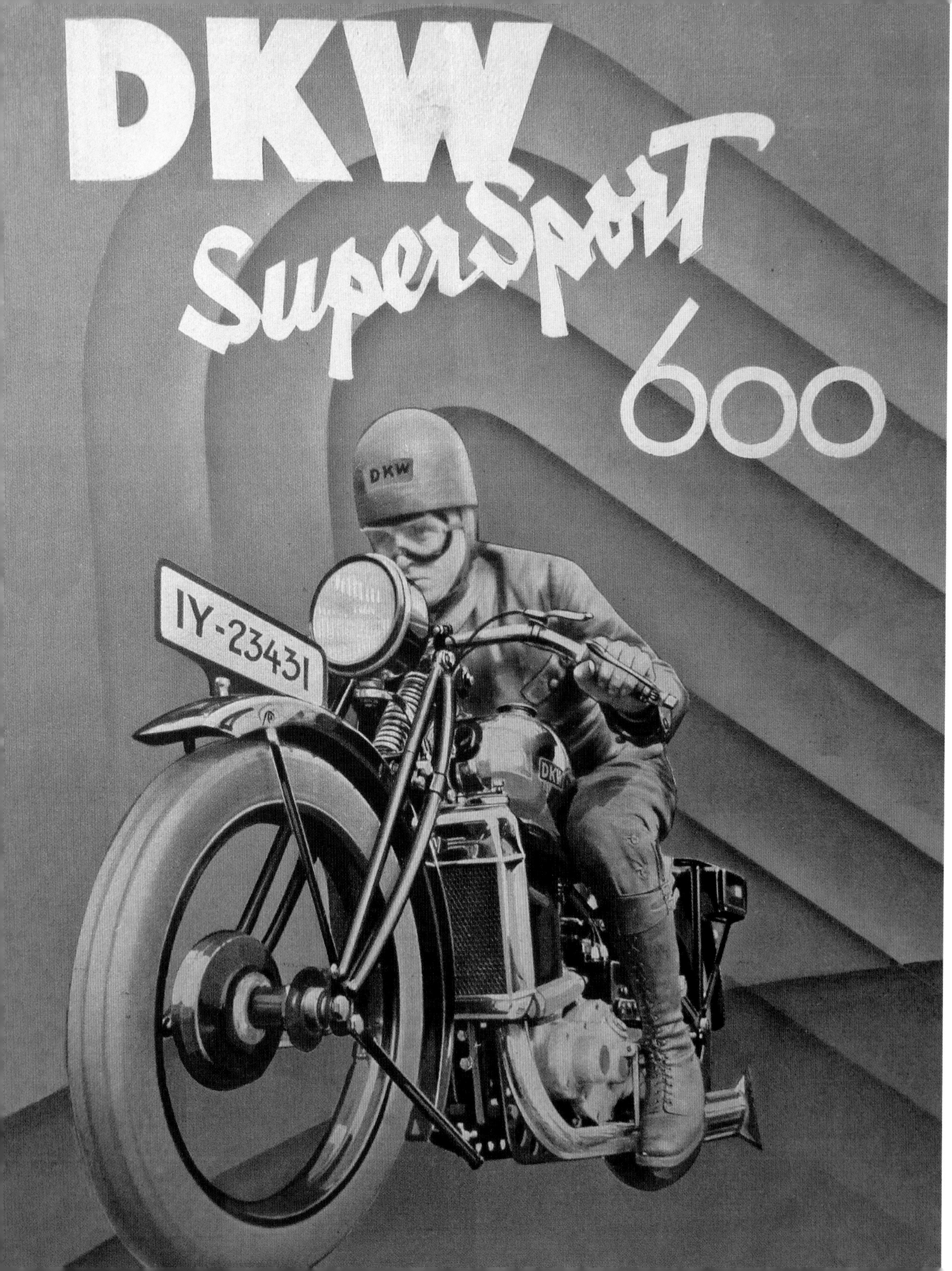
DKW
SuperSport
600
DKW
IY-23431
DKW

performance with a single's compactness and modest price. It changed the course of the British motorcycle industry: after World War II, every big factory made a parallel twin.

At Norton, there was drama when chief designer Walter Moore carried his blueprints for the CS1 OHC sports/racer under his arm to NSU, taking the same job at double the salary. He'd designed the "cricket bat" motor on his own time, and soon there were NSU roadsters and racers that looked identical to Nortons. Norton hired Arthur Carroll to redesign its OHC line, and he did the sensible thing: he copied features of the race-winning Velocette OHC motor. The Model 30 International was the foundation for hundreds of Grand Prix victories and evolved into the Manx, which is still in limited production today. At clubmen's events at Brooklands and at the Isle of Man, the Norton International was the machine to have, reliable and smooth with excellent road holding. By 1933 it had aluminum-bronze cylinder heads, exactly the sort of detail a Promenade Percy would covet—much as carbon-fiber bodywork does the same trick today.

The Rudge Ulster, a race replica with a four-valve motor, was as fast as anything on the road, barring a supersports V-twin. The Ulster Grand Prix appeared in 1929 as a road-equipped race replica of the first machine to lap a GP (the Ulster) at 80 miles per hour; it was an exceptional factory café racer and remained in production for the next ten years. Rudge had some of the best brakes in the industry from 1928 onwards, with 8-inch-diameter front and rear drums, a full inch larger than their closest competitors. Only Vincent-HRD had better brakes, as it doubled the drums on both front and rear wheels for its single-cylinder hot rods (the Meteor and Comet). In 1936, Vincent introduced the Rapide V-twin, a fever dream of a café racer that claimed the title of the world's fastest production motorcycle, with a top speed of 110 miles per hour. The Crocker Big Twin appeared the same year with the same top speed, but to our regret, they never raced against each other.

The unlikeliest factory café racer came from BSA, which had abandoned road racing after disastrous episodes in the early 1920s and now built solid, ordinary bikes. BSA's competition shop knew the 1937 Empire Star could be made to fly and so tuned one for retired star rider Wal Handley to ride at Brooklands. He duly reeled off 103-mile-per-hour

ABOVE: No 1930s trip to the seaside was complete without bright young Percys on modern, fast mounts looking to pillionize fairies in their bathing pajamas. *PT*

OPPOSITE: DKW built two-stroke GP racers of remarkable complexity, speed, and noise but also built fast two-stroke twins in the early 1930s, like this water-cooled 1934 600 SuperSport. *HMA*

ABOVE: The Norton M30 International was the hottest big single in Britain, a road-going replica of the factory racers that dominated the European GP scene. *PdO*

OPPOSITE: While the Velocette KTT was a production racer, it could be ordered with lights. This 1933 Mk4 KTT is nicknamed "the Mule" as it's been ridden on the toughest roads for decades. *NC*

Peugeot is arguably the oldest motorcycle company in the world, and in the 1930s, it built stylish Art Deco sports machines like this chromed-up 1936 515 model. *HMA*

laps, earning the coveted Gold Star badge for laps of 100-plus miles per hour during a race. BSA had the sense to offer a race replica in 1938, the M24 Gold Star, which had an aluminum cylinder and head, Amal TT racing carb, magnesium gearbox shell, and special silver/chrome paint job with a Gold Star tank decal. It was a genuine 100-mile-per-hour bike and among the finest factory café racers of the era, laying the foundation of the legendary postwar Gold Stars.

CUT DOWNS BECOME BOB JOBS

The United States was especially hard hit by the Great Depression, which devastated the motorcycle industry. Ignaz Schwinn, owner of Excelsior-Henderson, foresaw tough times and abruptly announced in 1931, "Gentlemen, today we stop." This left only two American motorcycle brands: Harley-Davidson and Indian. Factories had no budget for racing, so they worked with the American Motorcyclist Association (AMA) to create the

Class C series in 1934, permitting only cataloged motorcycles and parts, with 45-cubic-inch (750cc) side-valve engines competing against 500cc OHV machines. Class C racing reinforced domestic manufacturing trends toward side-valve V-twins, which seemed retrograde, but American engine tuners extracted shocking speeds from these "flatheads." How shocking? Rollie Free hit 111.6 miles per hour on an Indian Sport Scout with full road equipment on Daytona Beach in 1938 and 109.7 miles per hour on a Chief, lying flat on the tank with his legs stretched behind—a pose he would repeat in 1948 on a Vincent, in his bathing suit, to reach 150 miles per hour.

The cut down as a distinctly American café racer style evolved in the mid-1930s to become the bob job. Manufacturers had caught up with cut down chassis trends by the mid-1930s, making their frames shorter and lower, and tuners made better-handling, quicker-accelerating bikes by ditching the heavy front fender, "bobbing" the rear, and adding sports bars with a modest rise. A fast street bike in the United States was invariably a bob job in the 1930s and 1940s, and the style became (and remains) incredibly popular: vintage photos of period bob jobs abound, and all depict the American equivalent of a café racer. The only factory bob job of the period was the Crocker V-twin, built by Al Crocker from 1936 to 1941, which, with its top

ABOVE: The cut down was the original American custom style; this Harley-Davidson JDH has one cylinder blanked off, its frame shortened and lowered for better handling. *RO*

BELOW: Norton's CS1 was a sports roadster with extra chrome and wider fenders than the International, perfect for a well-dressed gent in his plus fours and brogues. *HMA*

Al Crocker stole the "world's fastest" crown in 1936 with his 110 miles per hour V-twins and offered a money-back guarantee for any rider ever beaten in a street race. *TV*

speed of 110 miles per hour, was the fastest American production motorcycle until 1958 (when the Harley-Davidson XLCH appeared). Crocker, like George Brough before him, was free to design the high-speed machine he knew riders wanted, but in a style they had developed themselves. Crocker used custom-bike cues with his paint schemes and sheet metal, although he was obliged to use a front fender—which many riders duly removed. Their rarity and speed made them legendary, and Crocker offered a street racer's guarantee: he'd return your money if an H-D or Indian beat you in a drag race! He never had to pay, because his bikes were the bomb.

American riding attire for the fast cyclist had evolved too, as racers were now required to wear protective leather gear and helmets. Sportier styles of leather jackets were becoming more common, especially as the zipper replaced buttons as the closure of choice. The most stylish riders found the diagonal-zip racing jacket to be ideal for street use and incorporated flying helmets and goggles, the outfit rounded off with cuffed dungarees and lace-up logger boots, just like racers wore. The quintessential biker jacket first appeared in the 1920s in Britain and in the 1930s in the United States, and, like the bob job, it became an enduring classic that remains a fashion staple to this day. An Yves Saint Laurent "biker" jacket might have extra stitches or studs, but it is clearly the same item American riders made famous before World War II.

THE BIG TWO

It took the wealth of the du Pont family to save Indian in 1930. E. Paul du Pont, founder and chairman of DuPont Motors, recognized that motorcycles had become leisure objects after the Ford Model T captured the transportation market. DuPont stylist Briggs Weaver reimagined Indians as Art Deco beauties in the mid-1930s, with twenty-four color options available; a 1936 Indian Chief resplendent in a five-color DuPont paint job remains one of the most beautiful motorcycles ever built. Tuners such as Rollie Free could extract 109 miles per hour from a Chief, but fast riders preferred the Scout, with its 750cc side-valve, semi unit-construction V-twin motor, which was faster than its bigger sibling. The Scout in its Daytona variant was a mainstay of Class C racing and thus became the speedman's ideal and the model for the bob job.

Harley-Davidson survived the 1930s without a change of ownership, although sales suffered terribly. That didn't stop the company introducing its first OHV V-twin in 1936, the EL "Knucklehead" (nicknamed for its lumpy rocker covers), which had plenty of speed potential—although it was slower than H-D's premium 1920s model, the JDH, which compounded the insult by being 90 pounds lighter. The factory didn't include the EL in its 1936 catalog, as it was concerned about potential warranty claims from heavy-handed riders and overhead valves. Those in charge needn't have worried, however, as the Knucklehead became legendary and could certainly be made to fly if one pitched its heavy tinware to make a bob job and raised the compression. Sports riders still tuned the side-valve 45-cubic-inch Model W, using speed secrets from Class C racing, and the typical

Edward Turner transformed a pokey single into a Tiger then stuffed a compact twin cylinder motor in its chassis, creating the super sports Triumph Tiger 100 in 1939. *HMA*

American café racer of the 1930s was a side-valve H-D bob job, its rider cool in a white tee, aviator shades, and a diagonal-zip leather jacket.

British and European motorcycles gathered on American shores by the 1930s, as Jack Sangster at Triumph actively sought exports and other dealers across the country brought in the Rudge Ulster, Norton International, Ariel Red Hunter, BMW R51, and Velocette KSS. These all appeared as racers on American tracks, modified for Class C racing. Their visibility in this series, especially at important venues such as Daytona (where Norton won in 1941), laid the ground for a huge export market for British companies after World War II. While there was an enormous rivalry between H-D and Indian, the fifteen-year separation from European racers was over, and fast riders were finding alternatives to heavy V-twins in lighter bikes from abroad.

OVER THERE

Postwar, fast machines in Europe included, as always, BMW, whose 500cc OHV R5 and R51 sports machines made a leap forward in handling, with the first proper telescopic forks and their light, tubular, all-welded frames. These replaced the Bauhaus grace of the R16 and R17 models, with their pressed-steel frames and 750cc OHV engines. DKW was the largest motorcycle factory in the world by the 1930s, and its two-stroke singles and parallel twins were popular and reasonably fast. It took a supercharger (or *Ladepumpe*) to make them successful racers, and in the 1930s, European factory racers were wildly different from street bikes, with OHC or DOHC singles, twins, and fours with superchargers and water cooling that were never seen on the street.

German riders adopted all-leather riding outfits in the 1930s as described in a 1934 issue of the *The Motor Cycle* by "Lederhosen" with envy:

I consider it the duty of every motorcyclist to make himself, as well as his machine, as serviceable and smart as his pocket allows. I have been motorcycling in Germany, and I consider much of the comfort and enjoyment of the various trips I made was due to the clothing I bought [there]. This kit consisted of a brown leather, double-breasted jacket, close-fitting, and with a high collar, like a military tunic,

Sam Oppie built a series of Harley-Davidson JDH cut downs in Seattle in the early 1930s. These were the fastest road bikes in the United States until the Crocker appeared in 1936. *RO*

fastening up under the chin. Zip-fastening sleeves and pock-ets were the useful decoration to the smart jacket. Below this I wore leather breaches, quite thinly lined, so that I got the pleasant feel of the leather and not a rough coarse blanket lin-ing, as in most racing breeches. These breeches, too, were cut on smart riding lines, and fit without a wrinkle into riding boots. The boots were pliable at the ankle, but had a long, stiff shafts which reached well up under the knee when the leg was bent in the running position. A pair of gloves with big, leather gauntlets, brightly polished at the beginning of the days run to match the boots, and a leather helmet completed the outfit. Since my return to England my motorcycling friends, among whom I count no Promenade Percys, have endorsed my own opinion of my all leather, all weather outfit.

The Percys, for their part, preferred Stormgard coats and Harris tweed plus-fours, but everyone was wearing khaki by the decade's end.

The 1936 Vincent-HRD Rapide was a doubled-up version of their Comet single co-designed by Philip Vincent and Phil Irving. Its top speed of 110 miles per hour stole the world's-fastest crown from the Brough Superior SS100. *PT*

THE 1940s:
THE BOOM AFTER
THE BOMB

There wasn't much left of the 1940s after World War II, but the immediate postwar period saw the sprouting of important trends in the United States and Britain while the rest of the world pulled itself from under the rubble. The war had sent millions of young men around the world, exposing them to people they'd otherwise never have encountered; a cross-pollination of ideas and close working quarters led to several immediate postwar developments, from new motorcycle designs to new customization trends to the idea of forming riding clubs with friends from the military. Decommissioned military motorcycles created a flood of ex–service machines available for cheap, which affected the immediate sales prospects of new motorcycles but put a lot of riders on the road. Many young men and women had also learned to ride as part of their military training—including the future Queen Elizabeth II herself as part of the Auxiliary Territorial Service, in February 1945 at age nineteen, aboard a BSA C10.

While the bob job was the dominant American café racer style, made using both Harley-Davidsons and Indians, the prewar trickle of motorcycles from Europe became a postwar flood as the United States became the world's largest marketplace for motorcycles. British machines were especially popular because they were fast and light, perfect for the increasingly popular off-road races all across the country. Class C racing rules were still in effect, meaning 500cc OHV bikes could compete against 750cc side-valve

OPPOSITE: This 1948 Norton International has plunger rear suspension—the "Garden Gate" frame—and excellent Roadholder forks. Still the hot ticket after 18 years' production. *HMA*

The calm before the storm: a BMW R51, a Triumph Speed Twin, and a Harley-Davidson Knucklehead in 1942, at a race in Devonshire, Canada. *TV*

racers. Billy Matthews won the 1941 Daytona racing a Norton International, which put fear in the hearts of the competition that American racing would go the way of European events, in which only OHC machines won races. That didn't prove the case, however, as Indian won the first two postwar Daytona 200s in 1947 and 1948, followed by four years of Norton victories. That raised British bike sales at a time when factories were desperate to raise American cash; thus began a two-decade conversation between British firms and their stateside customers. Americans demanded ever-larger motors with more power, which firms such as Triumph, Norton, BSA, and AMC were happy to supply. Most were immediately converted into either "desert sleds" for off-road racing or bob jobs for the street, the dominant style for speed-conscious riders—racers on the road in imitation of Class C machines.

Some bob jobs looked different by 1946, incorporating decorative elements into what had been a "strictly business" style. This was the point where the American custom motorcycles diverged, with performance-oriented machines remaining light and simple, and stylistic explorations evolving finally into the chopper by the late 1950s. The best-known stylist of the immediate postwar era was a young man named Kenneth Howard, who in 1945 worked at George Beerup's motorcycle shop using signwriting techniques he'd picked up from his father, Walker Howard, to improve the appearance of used motorcycles.

He decorated his own bob job 1936 Indian Scout with distinctive kicked-up exhaust pipes, handlebars on risers, and a smaller tank with a peculiar paint scheme: painted flames over chrome. For customers, he hand-lettered brand names or logos and added elaborate pinstriping, reminiscent of the nose art seen on World War II aircraft, with a hip, Beat flair. He was only sixteen when he started out, but demand for his paint work grew wild by the late 1940s, and his art spawned an enormous pop-culture movement of vehicle decoration. Under the nickname Von Dutch, his influence spread worldwide, and flame or speed-scalloped paint jobs and wild pinstriping formed part of an overall trend that became known as custom culture. Howard's creativity with paint was the origin point of custom motorcycles as we think of them today, and his peculiar bob job Indian seems to have bent the direction of custom motorcycles in America forever after. In the 1940s, bob jobs were still light and performance oriented, but the scene was set for a split between motorcycles modified primarily for style and racers on the road that took inspiration from the Grand Prix scene abroad.

Meanwhile, British manufacturers hastily added telescopic forks (first mass-produced by BMW in 1935) to their lineups but retained their rigid frames, barring Norton, which had been using plunger rear suspension since 1936. The need for a better-handling chassis was clear, as the racing world had been using rear springing for better road holding since the 1930s, and Velocette had invented the shock-damped swingarm frame in 1936. However, Velocette didn't bother to use that frame on its roadsters until 1953—unless you count Phil Irving's other immediate postwar design, the Velocette LE flat-twin of 1948, the polar opposite of his Vincent V-twins and a machine intended for the masses.

The original Norton Triumph hybrid—Triton—was built in 1942 by Rex McCandless in Ireland, who looked for better handling from his Triumph Tiger 100 racer. *VMCC*

ABOVE: It seemed every American bike got the bob job treatment, even British ones like this 1947 Velocette KSS seen in South Gate, California. *TV*

RIGHT: "Jack" had his business in order! This rare 1948 color photo shows the effort American riders put into customizing their fast machines, like this chromed-up 1947 Triumph Speed Twin bob job. *TV*

OPPOSITE: French chic on the Riviera returns after WWII, where even a humble 1948 Jawa Model 11 gives a stylishly dressed young woman a rakish air. *HMA*

This 1934 Indian Sport Scout, seen postwar, has a rider with classic style: cuffed denim, rolled-up sleeves, tattoos, and plenty of attitude. *TV*

Meanwhile, the release of the new Vincent-HRD Rapide Series B was a revelation. It was developed in secret during the war as a collaboration between Philip Vincent and Phil Irving, who sought to amend the problems of the Series A Rapide of 1936, which included an Albion clutch and gearbox too weak for the V-twin's urge and a mass of unsightly external oiling lines that gave rise to the nickname "the Plumber's Nightmare." The new Rapide took its forbear's place as the fastest production motorcycle in the world, though it would in turn be supplanted in 1948 by the Black Shadow; that model retained the title until the early 1970s, when Kawasaki's H2 Mach III 750cc two-stroke triple wheelied past the Vincent's creaky podium. The Black Shadow—or even better, a road-going Black Lightning—was the ultimate café racer, a machine that acquitted itself well on the race track but was built as a street machine for a rider who wanted the fastest motorcycle anywhere. Vincents lacked the 1920s elegance of a Brough Superior, but the war had destroyed the category of the "luxury motorcycle" it once occupied. The Vincent was, on the other hand, a technical tour de force, with an engine that remained the heart of fast motorcycling through the 1970s and the basis of new café racers to the present day, in Egli-framed incarnations.

The Isle of Man Clubman's TT, introduced in 1947, was intended to spur the development of road-going motorcycles, as only roadsters were allowed. "Clubman" had long been code for "café racer," and many factories dubbed their supersports roadsters thus in the 1930s. Club racing was popular at various British circuits, including Brooklands, which introduced a Clubman's Day race series in 1933, intended for standard production motorcycles, meaning fast street bikes, racers on the road, or café racers. The Clubman's TT proved very popular with riders, the public, and the press—it was an exciting series, as the racing was close, and the machines were relatable to the average motorcyclist. It was also an excellent opportunity for manufacturers to advertise the superiority of their cataloged motorcycles in speed, handling, and stamina. But there wasn't a universal embrace of Clubman's racing among manufacturers; factories that didn't offer racing bikes thought it a great opportunity to showcase their roadsters, while factories that did build racers (Velocette, Norton, AMC) worried that standard road bikes wouldn't hold up to the strains of racing. In truth, most factories did little to develop specific Clubman models, barring BSA and Matchless, and only BSA truly took up the gauntlet and developed its Gold Star series into the type of machine the organizers of Clubman's racing envisaged by the 1950s: fast and reliable, with great handling, brakes, and stamina.

In *The History of the Clubman's TT Races*, Fred Pidcock and Bill Snelling note that from the first 1947 race, "support from manufacturers, dealers, and accessories suppliers was by and large very strong indeed." The series proved, initially, fantastic for British manufacturers, and twelve different brands were represented the first year. The sight of these road-legal machines ridden flat out over the world-famous Isle of Man TT course stoked the fires of the café racer scene in Britain. Manufacturers developed Clubman models, and most were never raced, as is typical with race-replica models throughout history, but were no doubt ridden in imitation of their TT heroes in the postwar café racer explosion. Photos from the Clubman's TT provided a sterling example of how to look good while going fast, and ordinary riders in the thousands adopted TT riding gear

All bikes were fair game for customizing in the United States, including this 1948 Norton ES2 which was given high pipes and Velocette fishtails by "Jack." *TV*

and accessories: inverted handlebars, rear-set foot controls, racing carburetors and exhausts, and bum pads for a stretched-out riding position. The classic café racer style had been born, although it wasn't so named until the 1950s when the Clubman racing style merged with youth culture and rock 'n' roll, becoming wildly popular and visible to the world at large.

Many 1940s riders jumped ahead of the industry by converting their rigid-frame machines with a rear swingarm kit offered from 1946 by accessories firm Feridax, which had been developed by the McCandless brothers. They'd been tuning and racing their own machines since the 1930s and had purchased a hot new Triumph Tiger 100 to race in 1940—one of the very last civilian Triumphs before the war. While they liked the Triumph motor, the handling of its rigid frame was mediocre, so they installed the Tiger 100 motor into a racing Norton International chassis, which was slightly better but not revolutionary.

The Vincent Black Shadow claimed the title of world's fastest motorcycle for 35 years. This is its original Series B form, first offered in 1948 and featuring the large "coffee-can" speedometer.

That machine was the first Triton, built in 1942, a gorgeous piece of work and a fantastic café racer. But Rex McCandless had seen the Velocette factory racers with their air-damped shock absorbers (sourced from Dowty, which made aircraft landing gear) and modern swingarm frames. He built his own swingarm frame, cribbing ideas from the perimeter tube frame of the supercharged Gilera Rondine and using hydraulic shock absorbers from a Citroën car. The resulting special was dubbed the Benial (Irish for beast), which Rex considered "the best handling bicycle I ever made." He also developed a bolt-on rear subframe kit with hydraulic rear shocks, which speed-oriented riders clamored for once they'd seen them in action. Not interested in becoming manufacturers, the brothers sold the design to Feridax, and it became the hottest chassis kit of the 1940s. It would take over a decade before the next generation of chassis kits emerged, from the likes of the Rickman brothers and Egli, to cure the handling problems of 1950s machines.

ABOVE: For style and sophistication, there was no beating the Italians. This 1948 Parilla Tourist 250 had an overhead-camshaft motor and gorgeous lines. *HMA*

BELOW: While nearly invisible in the media, plenty of women rode in America after WWII, like Boozefighter "Little Little" on her Triumph Speed Twin bob job. *RO*

As an example of a 1940s speed merchant with a gift for writing, George Hylands described the café racer impulse in the immediate post-war era in his book *Fifty Years on British Bikes.* Hylands worked as a mechanic at a garage and owned a succession of interesting motorcycles, including an early Ariel Square Four and a brace

The rugged simplicity of a stripped-down mid-1930s Indian Scout, updated for racing in 1942 with newer Sport Scout cylinders, is the quintessential bob job—light and lean. Dig the Willys Woody bike hauler too! *TV*

of Velocettes, one of which he developed into a fierce 250cc, 105-mile-per-hour road burner, built for the sheer joy of taking high speeds on public roads. He described his first road test of a race-tuned Rudge Ulster that had been a prewar star:

> I thought I would give it a run as I hadn't even changed gear on it yet. Again it fired on the first turnover, so, advancing the mag up again, I shut off, and shoot off I nearly did. I had a few too many revs up because of a cold engine and when I took off it caught me unawares. When the multiplate clutch bit home, the Rudge took off with the front wheel lifting into the air! There was a couple walking along Golson Road and they both stopped to look. The lady had her hands over her ears. I must've been doing around 30 mph when I changed it to second gear and I soon found out that about 4 to 5000 revs were best for a nice smooth gear change. Into top at around 100 mph (about 5500rpm), I was really going now . . . at 6000 RPM on this gearing I must've been doing about 115 mph. I was flying along, much faster than the Square Four and a lot more stable.

One could feel the power. It was a real motorcycle. I felt elated and on shutting off I punched the air in sheer delight, as I had never ridden a racer like that one. It was brilliant and on pool petrol too, the octane was about 85—this was terrific! I didn't care what anyone said, for I was on a high.

Such a frank description of the joys of speed were rare, but every fan of café racers shares the feeling of being "on a high" at speed, with an engine singing beneath you and nothing but your skill to keep it all within the lines. Hylands described this feeling from a distance of fifty years as the memories of an old man, and they still feel fresh in the retelling, as they are honest and true. They also recount patently illegal behavior, which is perhaps why discretion kept them hidden for many decades. Such enthusiastic writing became increasingly common as the motorcycle industry offered ever faster, more competent motorcycles, and riders began sharing their experiences with a press that had grown more sensationalist after the war. The high-speed exploits of untamed youth would become a staple of the British tabloid press in the 1950s and 1960s, before menacing chopper gangs took their place as boogeymen in the late 1960s, at which point café racer riders came to be seen as wholesome by comparison.

A Harley-Davidson EL Knucklehead bob job, with its front fender moved out back for a stylish kick-up and whitewalls for days. *RO*

5

THE 1950s: CALL ME BY MY NAME

The café racer scene was strong in the early 1950s, and serious speed merchants got busy improving their essentially prewar machines with spring heels and tuning parts in Britain, or chrome and flashy paint in the United States. Speed-tuned road bike development might have proceeded in an orderly fashion had not fate and demographics intervened in the mid-1950s. A looming wave of young people—the baby boom—was fast approaching, and a rising tide of affluence meant more young people could afford motorcycles. As ever, youth was naturally attracted to speed, and fast motorcycles became more popular than ever as the decade progressed. What kicked it all sideways, though, was the arrival in the mid-1950s of rock 'n' roll. The raw sexuality of rock music seemed a perfect fit with two-wheeled thrills, its visceral appeal and propulsive beats matching the hyperventilated excitement of riding a fast motorcycle on a public road at 100 miles per hour.

Rock music fundamentally changed the subculture of speed around café racers, giving young riders a new identity and visibility as Rockers. Other music-oriented subcultures, such as Teddy Boys, didn't take to motorcycles, but for Rockers, music was inseparable from motorcycling. It was the first time a pop-culture music movement coincided with riding, and the two related subcultures shared visual cues in a

OPPOSITE: A peek behind the Iron Curtain in 1954, here we see a Jawa 175 and a rider clad all in leather, which must have been difficult to source in Czechoslovakia. *HMA*

ABOVE: The 1950 Vincent Rapide Series C was a sophisticated and very fast touring machine bristling with rider conveniences, and good for 110 miles per hour. *HMA*

OPPOSITE TOP: With rolled-up tee and tats in classic 1950s style, Roy B. Cook strikes a pose on his faithful Harley-Davidson Knucklehead bob job, complete with a small headlamp and Bates p-pad. *TV*

OPPOSITE BOTTOM: A 1952 Norton Model 88 twin in France. Rex McCandless' Featherbed frame was new and gave Manx handling to every engine in the Norton range. *HMA*

love for leather jackets. The black leather motorcycle jacket became a magical totem of youthful rebellion: it was modern-day armor for the knights of the road and those who wanted the vibe. In France, the *blousons noirs* were hoodlums, and media portrayals from America and Britain spread the same story to the world, as middle-class households were handed a new boogeyman in the form of juvenile delinquents. Fear of our own offspring—or exaggerated media portrayals of them—became a defining feature of the 1950s and 1960s, and young motorcyclists were an easy target, even among older riders, who showed nothing but contempt for the Rockers . . . forgetting that they, too, had once been young.

GROUND ZERO FOR ROCKERS: ENGLAND

The Rocker scene simply exploded from the mid-1950s and lasted over ten years. Rockers hung out at convenient roadside cafés on their favorite pathways out of city congestion, such as the Busy Bee, the Cellar, and the Ace Café, the latter of which became the best-known café racer hangout. Amazingly, given the full-throttle embrace of drugs in the 1960s, the rocker scene was squeaky clean, and riders eschewed even a pint of beer, preferring coffee or tea to keep sharp on the road. These cafés were open twenty-four hours and typically used by truckers; in the United States we'd call them truck stops, but in England they were called transport cafés. They were the only venues that accepted all comers (usually) and were tolerant of customers hanging around and spending little—most restaurants, pubs, and bars in this era were notorious for turning away motorcyclists, unless they were "biker bars." By the end of the 1950s, the rocker scene was in full bloom, with thousands of café racer enthusiasts congregating in the evenings at their favorite spots—which included, once again, the Southend seaport, just as in the 1930s. Some younger riders were well aware they were part of a long tradition and knew about Promenade Percys, or Bypass Berties, as they were called after the war.

There were new names for the new fashion as well—"coffee-bar cowboys" and "ton-up boys." Their bikes were called "coffee bar racers," which by the end of the 1950s became simply café racers ("caff racers" in proper working-class slang). The term was meant

to distinguish (and shame) these riders for not having the discipline work out their speed urges to the racetrack. The ton in ton-up boy, of course, meant 100 miles per hour, and author Mick Duckworth notes the term likely came from Cockney dialect, in which £100 was a "ton," as was 100 points on a pinball machine. A 100-mile-per-hour top speed had been the measure of a top-tier sporting motorcycle since the 1920s, when George Brough made it the selling point of his SS100, and other manufacturers did their best to offer TT replicas, Ulsters, and Super Sports that could approach the ton while remaining road legal. Very few machines could reach 100 miles per hour before World War II unless one raised the compression, removed the muffler, and paid attention to the carburetion, which café racer fans had been doing for years. The very best Norton Internationals and Rudge Ulsters could be so tuned, as could a Triumph Tiger 100 if the endcaps were removed from their mufflers, creating megaphones. Postwar, most clubman's machines were capable of 100 miles per hour, and ton-up boys were renowned for riding their hot machines to their maximum, taking known bends as fast as they could manage—sometimes with dire consequences.

The parking lots of transport cafés could be chaotic in the evenings, as riders turned up after work to hang out, have a quick meal, and hang around with friends. Spontaneous fast rides were called burn-ups, and riders sized up

ABOVE: The ultimate factory café racer? The 1956 BSA DB34 Gold Star Clubman, a racer on the road if ever there was one, and a thing of great beauty. *HMA*

OPPOSITE: Alan Shepherd crawls under the paint to come third on a 350cc Norton International in the 1956 Clubman's TT, when the Inter was no longer catalogued. *HMA*

other riders' skills and challenged visitors to a race if they shot their mouths off. It was reminiscent of chivalric horsemanship contests of ancient days, with boastful young men (and it was typically men who boasted) being put to task with a challenge of skill. There were also women motorcyclists who frequented transport cafés, some of them quite talented riders who gained a reputation of their own, and the respect of male riders. Mick Duckworth does an excellent job documenting them, and the rest of the scene at the Ace Café, in his book Ace Times, the most comprehensive examination of the rocker era and its resonant aftermath.

BRITISH INDUSTRY: BIGGER AND FASTER

The Clubman's TT was intended to spur technical development of motorcycles through experience gained in taking ordinary machines to their limits. In reality, very few factories took production racing seriously besides BSA, which developed its Gold Star line specifically to win Clubman's racing events. The rest of the British industry stalled in developing the fast and durable machines such racing demanded, including Norton, whose International model did well in the early Clubman's series but had hardly evolved since 1931. Only the adoption of the Featherbed frame gave the Inters a handling advantage from 1951 and kept them in the picture. Because BSA seemed the only manufacturer developing the Gold Star line for the Clubman's TT, the race eventually became a Goldie benefit.

By 1950, the Junior Clubman's TT (350cc) leaderboard was dominated by BSAs, and by 1954, the Senior (500cc) event was too. In the 1955 race, the first twenty-seven places in the Junior Clubman's were Gold Stars, while the Senior race was totally dominated by BSAs from 1955. We'll never know how the final version of the BSA Clubman Gold Star—the DBD34—would have fared, because the race was cancelled for 1957, the year that model was introduced. BSA carried on building the Gold Star Clubman through 1963, because demand from racers had been superseded by a clamor from fast road riders for the ultimate road burner, with its amazing looks, excellent handling, and 110-mile-per-hour top speed. The DBD34 is the ne plus ultra of British factory café racers from

Old and new bob jobs: a post-1948 Harley-Davidson FL Panhead and pre-1948 Knucklehead. Both are pictured here with classic American style such as cuffed jeans and engineer's boots. *TV*

A race-kitted Triumph Tiger 100 in France at the Bol d'Or in 1954, complete with sprung hub and extra lights for night riding in this 24-hour production race. *HMA*

the 1950s and a thing of exquisite beauty in its purposefulness. Its perfection was achieved by evolution rather than design. The swelling chrome tank and silver paint with red pinstripes were standard for the Gold Star line from 1937, but somehow these features looked best on the final version, with its big-fin aluminum cylinder and head, clip-on handlebars, and huge 1.5-inch Amal GP carburetor. BSA provided a warning to prospective buyers in its catalogs that "the Clubman's model Gold Star has been developed for competition in road and short circuit events, and its specification is such that it is neither intended nor suitable for road use as a touring motorcycle." Somehow this only confirmed the Gold Star was exactly the right machine for the road!

The Gold Star was nearly equaled in both grace and speed by the Triumph Tiger T100C, which was a lovely machine. The Competition Tiger had fine-pitch finning on its aluminum engine with twin carbs, a 1-gallon oil tank, and a tachometer as standard but retained a rigid rear frame and heavy "sprung hub." It took until 1955 for Triumphs to gain swing-arm frames, and while Edward Turner was a masterful stylist, his 1950s Triumphs had dubious handling and tied themselves into knots in hard use. According to *The History of the Clubman's TT Races* (Pidcock & Snelling), Turner's own development team knew of these problems and built a

OPPOSITE: Belying expectations, Anke-Eve Goldmann was a schoolteacher who adored fast motorcycles and rode like the wind. This is the second BMW R69 built, with an optional Hoske long-distance tank. *TV*

LEFT: A café racer's dream: the factory 1954 Norton Domiracer, with highly tuned Model 88 engine and Manx chassis. It's sexy from every angle. *HMA*

BELOW: Goldmann was 2 meters tall and designed her own full leathers with a diagonal zip, made by Harro. One-piece racing suits were de rigeur by the mid-1950s. *TV*

ABOVE: The Italians did it better, making sophisticated overhead-camshaft road legal roadburners built like jewelry, as with this 1957 MV Agusta Squalo. *HMA*

RIGHT: Goldmann in 1958 rides on her BMW R69 with a Peel fairing for high-speed riding, at which she excelled, although she was not allowed to race. *TV*

prototype with an altered steering-head angle and proper weight distribution, which cured the handling problems. But Turner was enraged, claiming he'd never experienced the problems claimed for his design, and thus they were not corrected until Turner witnessed the death of a competitor in the United States when the rider broke his Triumph TR6T frame in an off-road race. The next year, Triumph revealed an improved frame, which was at least adequate for fast riding, meaning the power developed by the 650cc Bonneville was no longer frightening to exploit in corners.

"LIKE RIDING A FEATHER BED"

While the McCandless brothers had sold their swingarm conversion design to Feridax, the chassis of their Benial Triumph racer, designed in 1941, pointed the way forward for the whole industry. Rex McCandless and his business partner Artie Bell approached Norton to offer the manufacturer the design. They built a prototype Norton with a bent-tube, double-loop, all-welded frame made of lightweight steel, incorporating car dampers at the rear. It looked radically different from any motorcycle then built and was a leap forward in motorcycle chassis design. Norton staff loved it, but the factory was reluctant to manufacture it, as the all-welded frame was an unknown quantity. McCandless described how he finally convinced Norton (including racing manager, Joe Craig) of his frame's superiority on a test on a section of the Isle of Man course in 1949:

The ubiquitous D. Lewis Bronx jacket seen here in 1956, the classic Rocker style, was both a tuxedo for any occasion and armor for battle on the road. *LL*

"Artie Bell was on my bike, ultimately christened the Featherbed by Harold Daniell. Geoff Duke was on a Garden Gate and both had Works engines. [Norton director] Gilbert Smith, Joe Craig and I stood on the outside of the corner at Kate's Cottage. We could hear them coming from about the 33rd [milestone]. When Geoff came through Kate's he was needing all the road. Artie rode around the outside of him on full bore, miles an hour faster, and in total control. That night Gilbert Smith and I had a good skinful."

When Norton debuted the Featherbed frame in 1950, it set the gold standard for motorcycle chassis design for twenty-five years.

THE THRILLING *Scramblers*

THE MACHINE **EVERYONE** WANTS

Royal Enfield CRUSADER *Sports*

| OUTPUT 17 B.H.P. (approx.) | MAXIMUM SPEED 80 M.P.H. (approx.) | A REALLY STRIKING 250 | HANDSOME AND SPORTING APPEARANCE |

The 250 with maximum performance

DUCATI MECCANICA BOLOGNA

DUCATI 175 *Sport*

caratteristiche principali

175 cm³ - 4 tempi - distribuzione con valvole in testa a V, comandate da un albero a cammes in testa.
Consumo benzina lt. 3,2 per 100 Km.
Velocità massima circa 130 Km/h. - Cambio a 4 velocità.

Riders and racers looking for a handling advantage turned to the Norton frame, which had given the aging Manx single-cylinder OHC motor a new lease on life. There was one racing clan that didn't need the Featherbed chassis, however: 500cc Formula car racers, who used the Manx motor in Cooper and other "cigar" race cars, leaving a Norton chassis spare. The first to fill this void was John Surtees, who worked at Vincent in 1954 and built a Black Lightning motor from factory parts to install in a Norton racing chassis. The resulting machine was the first NorVin, which was road-registered for testing, making one hell of a 150-mile-per-hour café racer. Surtees intended to race the beast but joined the Norton factory race team instead. The cat was out of the bag, though, as images of his NorVin were published widely, and imitations soon appeared on the streets, built from roadster or racer Norton frames and displaying a bewildering variety of detail finishes. All NorVins are seriously badass, and all share the distinction of being the fastest café racers of all, a title they held right through the 1970s.

The Featherbed frame could accept almost any-sized motor, and soon just about anything was stuffed inside. Rex McCandless himself tried a four-cylinder Norton-Fiat in 1947; others installed OHC car engines from Hillman and NSU, and even Rover aluminum V-8 motors on occasion. Far more common, however, was the ubiquitous Triumph twin engine, which was cheap on the secondhand market and could be tuned easily with the explosion of aftermarket parts available to service young café racer fans. While the first Triton was built by Rex McCandless circa 1943, the earliest Featherbed Tritons were built in the mid-1950s, perhaps inspired by John Surtees. These undoubtedly used genuine Manx racing chassis, with magnesium wheel hubs and aluminum bodywork. As the Triton grew more popular in the 1960s, roadster chassis were used, with heavier tubing and ordinary single-leading-shoe brakes, but by then, an enormous aftermarket industry had sprung up in response to the incredible demand for café racer parts.

The Triton and NorVin were absolute classic café racers that, though rarely actually raced, had incredible street cred as bona fide performance machines built for the purpose. As all were custom motorcycles, no two were ever quite alike, and their build quality varied widely. The purest and most essential examples were the first ones of the 1950s, built from a genuine racing Manx chassis and retaining the perfect Norton aluminum bodywork and racing wheels. These capitalized on the functional perfection of the Manx, which was an ideal aesthetic and the very image most café racer builders sought to imitate, whether they used a Norton chassis or not.

Another excellent choice for riders with spare engines was the BSA chassis, which had been developed for Clubman racing with the Gold Star but

OPPOSITE TOP LEFT: The Harley-Davidson XLCH could be ordered in road or scrambler form. They weighed 450 pounds with lights, had 50 horsepower in 1957, and was Harley's fastest roadster for decades. *HMA*

OPPOSITE TOP RIGHT: Factory café racers were sometimes more sheep than wolf, like this 1959 Royal Enfield Crusader Sports, a 250 single with dropped 'bars as the only sporting feature. *TV*

OPPOSITE BOTTOM: The 1958 Ducati 175 Sport had a jelly-mould tank, dual mufflers, clip-ons, and alloy rims as standard and generally showed the way forward for racers on the road. *JG*

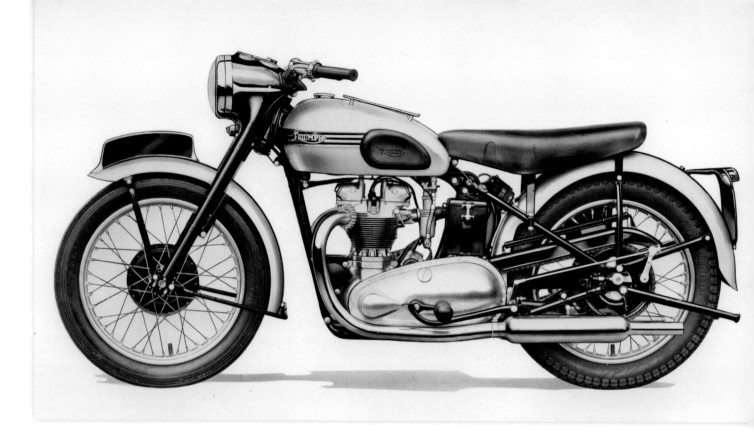

This 1952 Triumph Tiger 100 could be ordered with a full race kit for Clubman racing but looked fast in totally standard trim, as with this catalog shot. The fine-pitch fins on the aluminum cylinders and head make this the prettiest Triumph motor ever. *HMA*

was basically identical across the twin-cylinder and single-cylinder range by 1954. It was also a double-loop, welded-up frame but used a single spine tube, with a double cradle curving under the motor and back to the seat nose. The BSA frame had race-proven handling, and its open construction made an easy swap for a Triumph motor, making the TriBSA a popular café racer. It might seem strange to replace one parallel twin motor with another to create a café racer, but the Triumph motor had the advantage of a larger aftermarket tuning-parts industry and considerable experience among owners who tuned them for racing. By 1954, the BSA Road Rocket and later Super Flash models were the equal of the Triumph Tiger 110 in performance, with 42 horsepower and a top speed of 110 miles per hour, using high-compression pistons and a single racing Amal TT carb. That should have been enough to satisfy any road-burning youth, but the perception was that Triumphs were faster, and café racers, as we've demonstrated over the decades, have always been about perception as much as actual performance.

THE ITALIAN JOB

Let's just be clear about the evolution of café racers in the 1950s: while the British are credited with going mad for racers on the road in that decade, it was the Italians who got there first. While British decorum saw that country's industry tiptoe around the red-blooded erotic desire of young riders for fast machines, to Italians this was simply normal, and their motorcycle industry followed suit by offering exactly the machines riders wanted, with no excuses. But the Italian bikes were typically 250cc and under in the 1950s, and regardless of the fact that many Italian small-capacity café racers were actually faster than 650cc parallel twins by the 1960s, most performance-oriented riders wanted a big bike. Compensation? Posing? Yes. But not all fans of café racers needed such, and they were happy to "do the ton," as hitting 100 miles per hour became known, on a very fast machine of small capacity, which in the 1950s would have been Italian.

Italy revved up in the 1950s as the economy pulled itself from the rubble of World War II, and the many factories once building armaments turned to making small motorcycles to survive, much like in Germany and Japan. Italians do things differently, however, and as soon as it was able, the country channeled its bellicose energies into racing, especially on two wheels. Despite the majority of riders still needing basic transport and therefore purchasing utilitarian machines, the popularity of long-distance road races determined the range-leading models for every factory, which was a racer with lights. Italy embraced competitions such as the Milano–Taranto and Mille Miglia, which required its racing motorcycles to be road legal with full road equipment—especially lights for night riding. Thus, unique among the world's motorcycle-building nations, the Italians understood the café racer as the ideal motorcycle and a goal for nearly every rider.

By 1959, the BSA DBD34 Gold Star Clubman was a perfected machine built for a purpose—to dominate the Clubman's TT—which made it one of the ultimate factory café racers of all time. *PT*

The most popular engine capacity in Italy was 125cc, which seems small to modern eyes but was aspirational to the vast majority of riders in a country dragging itself from poverty. Racing in all capacities, from 50cc to 500cc, was extremely popular, but for most, the 125cc class was the field of dreams: relatable and semi-affordable. While the larger factories (Moto Guzzi, Gilera, Benelli, Bianchi) built exotic multicylinder Grand Prix racers for the World Championships, which Italians were allowed to enter starting in 1950, a hundred other factories built small-capacity racers in increasingly sophisticated specifications. Examples include FB Mondial, MV Agusta, and Ducati, which all built lovely OHC singles for road and racing that were beautifully engineered and gem-like in their aesthetic perfection. The hottest models were relatively expensive, especially abroad, where an Italian 175cc OHC supersports machine might cost more than a big 650cc British twin.

Italian racing machines dominated the Grand Prix circuit by the mid-1950s, but their increasingly exotic specifications, with multiple cylinders and dual-OHC heads, were unavailable to road riders. Their external details, though, informed café racers the world over, with their jelly-mold, body-hugging tanks and dustbin fairings becoming the apex style of the 1950s and early 1960s. As much as the Norton Manx and AJS 7R inspired café racer builds, so did the Gilera and MV Agusta 4-cylinder racers.

There were other fast machines built in Europe in the 1950s, including the first BMW with a top speed of 100 miles per hour: the R68, still using the plunger frame BMW had adopted in 1938. Perhaps the ultimate 1950s café racer was a BMW; a factory job built to congratulate rider Walter Zeller on his second place in the GP World Championships—a road-going RS 255 Kompressor with lights! Horex singles were tuned by the likes of Fritz Egli and made into café racers, as were Adler two-stroke twins and even NSU Super Max singles. In the mid-1950s, NSU totally dominated 250cc Grand Prix racing with its ultrasophisticated twin-cylinder DOHC Rennmax racers, and BMW dominated sidecar racing with its OHC flat-twin Rennsport engines, but such Grand Prix technology would take decades to reach the road. The distance between road and racer began to narrow only in the 1980s, closing entirely by the 1990s, when it became possible to buy a road-legal motorcycle that was the near-equal of a factory racing job. Riders of the 1950s could only dream about bikes of exotic specification under their control, so they made do, as riders always have, modifying what was available for more speed.

ABOVE: A beautiful and fast machine, this Matchless G11 Clubman tests at the MIRA banked track, where it easily clocked 105 miles per hour. *HMA*

OPPOSITE: In 1959, Triumph added a racing cylinder head with twin carburetors and a hot camshaft to its 650cc twin and named it for the Bonneville Salt Flats, where Johnny Allen had taken a streamliner powered by a Tiger 110 to a world record 214.4 miles per hour in 1956. *PT*

6

THE 1960s: CAFÉ RACERS AROUND THE WORLD

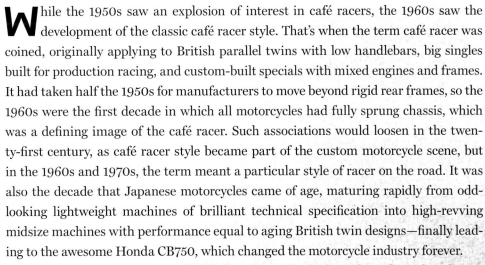

While the 1950s saw an explosion of interest in café racers, the 1960s saw the development of the classic café racer style. That's when the term café racer was coined, originally applying to British parallel twins with low handlebars, big singles built for production racing, and custom-built specials with mixed engines and frames. It had taken half the 1950s for manufacturers to move beyond rigid rear frames, so the 1960s were the first decade in which all motorcycles had fully sprung chassis, which was a defining image of the café racer. Such associations would loosen in the twenty-first century, as café racer style became part of the custom motorcycle scene, but in the 1960s and 1970s, the term meant a particular style of racer on the road. It was also the decade that Japanese motorcycles came of age, maturing rapidly from odd-looking lightweight machines of brilliant technical specification into high-revving midsize machines with performance equal to aging British twin designs—finally leading to the awesome Honda CB750, which changed the motorcycle industry forever.

That the café racer image solidified in the 1960s had much to do with independent accessories suppliers. A profitable industry had sprung up to sell tuning parts, bodywork kits, and whole machines in the café racer style; now anyone could alter a standard machine to look like a racer on the road. Famous names such as Dunstall,

OPPOSITE: The 1964 BSA Lightning Clubman was a factory café racer built long after the Clubman's TT was finished but when production racing flourished. *HMA*

ABOVE: This photo of a young Rocker on his BSA Gold Star taken by Henry Grant in 1961 at the Ace Café served as the cover image for Jonny Stuart's seminal book *Rockers*. PK

RIGHT: Ace Café regular Jenny Burton and friends are pictured here in a rare color shot by Henry Grant in 1961, which ran as a cover for *Today Magazine* article, "*Live Fast, Love Hard, Die Young*." PK

Rickman, Tickle, Petty, and Hyde were happy to supply racing parts for street bikes, while companies like Fi-Glass and Avon supplied fiberglass tanks and fairings. Magazine ads from a dozen more companies offered exhaust systems, lightweight bodywork, aluminum controls, clip-ons, racing carbs, racing brakes, bump-stop seats, triple clamps, and on and on. Tuning shops offered polished rocker arms, hot cams, big-valve conversions, high-compression pistons, aluminum timing and magneto gears, and much more. Riders "added lightness" to everything (to quote Colin Chapman at Lotus), and parts were drilled out whether or not it added performance. Then again, Berkeley café racer guru Paladin said, "Of course it makes no sense to drill your Triumph's timing gears, but if you're proud of your work, you're more likely to look inside your motor, which is a good thing."

The 1960s café racer became an international style, with riders in every country building similar-looking machines. American, British, Australian, European, and even Japanese café racer fans bought British, German, or Japanese bikes and converted them to look like racers. Sometimes Harley-Davidson Sportsters were modified too; the XLCH Sportster was the company's fastest production bike ever and the speed equal of

The Leather Boys

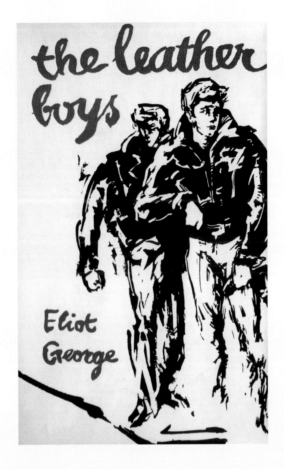

The Wild One inspired a wave of youth exploitation films in the 1950s featuring bored middle-class kids making trouble or becoming werewolves. Films about British rocker culture were also over-dramatized and badly acted, but *The Leather Boys* stands out as the only film attempting to capture the lived experience of working-class British bikers. Part of the kitchen sink movement of realistic film-making, it was shot with few professional actors and a lot of actual rockers who hung out at the Ace Café in London, where much of the action was filmed. It was based on the book of the same name by Gillian Freeman, which was published in 1961 under the pseudonym Eliot George (an inversion of George Eliot—Mary Ann Evans's nineteenth-century nom de plume while writing *Middlemarch* and *Silas Marner*). Freeman's book was nowhere near the literature of her inverted namesake, being a quick-read pulp novel whose overleaf exclaimed, "The leather boys are the boys on the bikes, the boys who do a ton on the by-pass. For their expensive machines, they need expensive leather jackets. They are an aimless, lawless, cowardly and vain lot with a peacock quality to their clothes and hair style."

Freeman adapted her book for the 1964 film, altering the story line significantly, as the book treated crime, violence, and homosexuality with a frankness that was far ahead of its time. The film starred Rita Tushingham as teenage bride Dot and Colin Campbell as her husband, Reggie; their relationship becomes a love triangle, with Reggie the prize and Pete (Dudley Sutton) Dot's unexpected rival. Reg rides a Triumph Tiger 110 at the film's start, and graduates to a new Bonneville while Pete buys a Norton 650SS. The pair enjoy fast times at the Ace Café, with fantastic shots of period café racers in the parking lots and on the road. Actual motorcyclists will cringe at a long-distance race featuring a 250cc Ariel Leader keeping up with a Bonnie and a Dommie, but in general the film is surprisingly authentic in its depiction of the Ace Café scene and the social standing of the rockers as generally young, working-class boys and girls.

In the novel, the suggested relationship between Reg and Pete (Dick in the book) is consummated, and Reg is murdered by their gang of thieves for committing a robbery on their own. In the film, Reg and Pete's relationship is innocent, but the implication of an intimate male bond is spat out by Dot—"Men? You look like a couple of queers." It turns out at the end of the film, after the boys have sold their motorcycles to ship out of Cardiff as merchant seamen, that Pete is well known to gay sailors; Reg, confused and ultimately straight, walks away disappointed. The moral of the story: never sell your café racer!

LEFT: The Honda CB92 was a small, high-revving gem of a motorcycle, a proof of the concept that sophisticated engineering could be made cheap and reliable. *RV*

BELOW: Flat out! Velocette Director Bertie Goodman tests a 1960 Venom Clubman with full race kit at 106 miles per hour. The next year he would ride one for 24 hours at 100.4 miles per hour. *TV*

Britain's fastest production bike, the Dunstall Norton Atlas. Both bikes were tested at 125 miles per hour by the press. American journalists used the term café racer to describe a racer on the road by 1963, and the term was in common parlance among motorcyclists everywhere. Magazines were happy to cover both well-made home-built specials and the products of independent café racer companies such as Dunstall or Rickman. They also featured riders such as Zach Reynolds, heir to the Reynolds tobacco fortune, who ordered a Norton Atlas café racer direct from Paul Dunstall and a Velocette Thruxton from American importer Lou Branch and was happy to line up his enviable collection for photographers. Steve McQueen owned a Dunstall Dominator too.

INSTALL DUNSTALL

Paul Dunstall stuffed a race-tuned Norton Dominator engine into a Manx-style chassis in 1957 and raced it successfully. Demand for replicas meant he offered his first catalog of parts for tuning Nortons by 1961. By 1966 he was certified as an official motorcycle manufacturer and participated in production racing events, winning the 1968 Production TT. The Dunstall Dominator was based on the Norton 650SS model with Manx styling, and the engine could be ordered specially tuned to easily give a top speed of 120 miles per hour. *Motor Cycle* magazine was enamored of the Dunstall in May 1965: "How about this for

BELOW: Paul Dunstall sold parts and whole motorcycles in various states of tune. The base model Dunstall Dominator was good for 120 miles per hour and featured gorgeous Manx styling. *SMW*

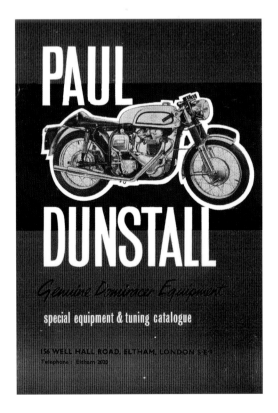

The future has arrived. The Suzuki X6 Hustler, which handled well and looked fast sitting still, was good for nearly 100 miles per hour and was stone reliable, simple, cheap. *HMA*

a dream? Two-miles-a-minute top whack; out-accelerate a Manx Norton; cover a standing-start quarter-mile in sprint time; yet easily restart on a 1 in 4 gradient; tick-tock idling at 500 rpm. This dream travels under the name, Dunstall Dominator. On road and track it provided me with some of the most scintillating miles I've ever covered on a production bike. Draped in Dunstall goodies, it attracted almost embarrassing attention, not only from youngsters, but mums and dads. I even lit up many an old grandfather's eyes. This lavishly bedecked Norton is one of the most arresting creations ever to grace a road." In 1967, the Dunstall Atlas with 750cc motor was tested at 131 miles per hour, and the Dunstall Commando ended up with 70 horsepower at the rear wheel, which made for spectacular performance.

NOTHING AS FAST AS A VINCENT

Despite the Dunstall's hot spec, it was still not as fast as a bike that had stopped production ten years prior: the Vincent Black Shadow. Regardless of its potential for speed tuning, the Vincent chassis, designed in 1945, was made obsolete by Norton's Featherbed frame. Vincents remained the world's fastest production motorcycles for nearly thirty years because their engine was superb, but their handling was another matter. The first person to address the handling deficiencies was future world champion (on two and four wheels) John Surtees, who shoehorned a Black Lightning engine into a Norton Manx racing chassis, creating the first NorVin in 1954. The big V-twin lump looked perfect in the Manx chassis, and other builders followed Surtees's example. The NorVin was the king of café racers until the late 1960s,

Above: 59's breakdown van is on call - and John Waller (below right) is the No. 1 driver Below left: Member Roy Teather at the Palace

ABOVE LEFT: A Henry Grant photo of Rockers at the Ace Café circa 1961 with racy Triumphs and empty cups of tea. These riders are ready for a burn up on the North Circular road. *PK*

ABOVE RIGHT: The 59 Club offered a place for London's Rockers to hang out, with added benefits like a breakdown service by Father Shergold himself! This spread is from *Link*, the club's magazine. *TV*

LEFT: Cecil Richards, on his BSA Super Rocket with its 666 number plate, sits beside Father Bill Shergold of the 59 Club at the Ace Café. *AC*

500 thruxton

Inheritor of the mantle of world's hottest single cylinder café racer, the Velocette Thruxton won the 1967 Production TT and was very fast and durable. *HMA*

when Swiss racer Fritz Egli entered the scene and gave new hope to fans of British iron.

In the mid-1960s, Egli campaigned a hot Vincent twin that had 75 horsepower at the rear wheel but was a pig to manage around corners. He decided a large-diameter backbone tube frame would be nearly indestructible and could carry the engine oil. His frame was finished in 1967, its straightforward tube spine attached to a tripodal subframe for the swingarm pivot, shock mounts, and seat platform. Egli built two machines in time for the 1967 Zurich Motorcycle Show, a road racer and a café racer. With no money for a booth, he snuck his machines into the exhibition hall, parking them in a corner by some decorative plants, and balanced them on wood blocks. The bikes looked sensational and sent ripples through the café racer world for their sexy lines and potential for very high performance. Egli used the most advanced components available for his chassis, all Italian: Ceriani road race forks, Fontana magnesium or Campagnolo mechanical disc brakes (for the racer), and Borrani alloy rims. The Anglo-Swiss-Italian mix soon proved its worth in competition, when Egli himself won the Swiss Hillclimb Championship in 1968. It was a fairy-tale start for this always-tiny business, and Egli built about two hundred of his Vincent specials before shifting his attention to Japanese motors as the 1960s eased into the 1970s.

SPECIAL BLENDS

Less professional hybrids than Egli's included thousands of Tritons, which could be seen using unit-construction Triumph engines after 1963 with no loss of its appeal. Triumph had cured its handling quirks by then, but the compelling style of the Triton was reason enough to build one, and the variety of their final spec seemed limitless. But Triumph wasn't the only motor to fill the Featherbed's vacancy; other specials were built with 1,000cc Ariel Square Four motors, BSA Gold Stars, Velocette Thruxtons, BSA twins, and Hillman Imp or NSU Prinz engines. While Norton Roadholder forks were still excellent, owners could upgrade the front brakes with aftermarket twin-leading-shoe backplates from John Tickle; a four-leading-shoe brake from Robinson; or, if going all out, one of the many Italian suppliers of aftermarket magnesium racing brakes, such as Fontana, Grimeca, or Oldani. Special-building with the Featherbed frame was a popular pastime in the 1960s, and some builders became small producers of their ideal machines. These included the Viscount, a limited-production NorVin, and the Healey Four with its Ariel Square Four Mark II engine.

THE RICKMAN-ANYTHING

The Rickman brothers built the most advanced, lightest, and best-styled motocross chassis kits in the world starting in 1960. The next logical step was to produce a road-racing chassis, and by 1963 the brothers were offering a longer and more stable twin-loop Featherbed-ish frame with a gorgeous set of Mitchenall fiberglass bodywork. As suitable racing engines weren't available "loose," the chassis was designed to fit a multitude of powerplants, and Triumph, Matchless, and Velocette engines soon found new homes in shiny nickel frames. The Rickman racing chassis was an immediate hit, and a road-legal version was available by 1964. The Rickman-Triumph street model was a stunning machine and is widely acknowledged as one of the ultimate 1960s café racers, being a perfect combination of styling and performance. Even with a standard Bonneville engine installed, its light weight, excellent suspension and brakes, and rock-solid handling made it a machine that delivered on the road. The Rickman-Triumph proved its quality when

The Royal Enfield Continental GT was a factory café racer styled for young riders with all the right components derived from 1950s Clubman racing and was a very popular machine. *PT*

The Girl on a Motorcycle

Marianne Faithfull plays Rebecca in the 1968 film *Girl on a Motorcycle*, based on the book *La Motocyclette*; her character is based on Anke-Eve Goldmann. *TV*

The one-piece zip-up leather racing suit has been the legal minimum standard for protective competition gear for over sixty years, but the question of who invented it has long been subject to debate. Movie-star-handsome Geoff Duke made the one-piece famous in 1951 after his local tailor, Frank Barker, sewed one up to Duke's instruction. He'd already been wearing a one-piece fabric undergarment beneath his two-piece leathers, made up by a ballet specialist in London, which elicited a few "ribald comments" from his teammates. I'll grant nobody else wore a ballet onesie while racing in 1949, but the director of Veloce Ltd., Bertie Goodman, was already wearing his own one-piece leather suit in 1949. Duke certainly knew who Bertie was—the rare factory director who actually raced motorcycles—so the idea of the one-piece suit was around, as they say.

Nobody knows who the first female rider wearing a one-piece might have been, but we certainly know who, like Duke, made it famous. Anke-Eve Goldmann was riding and competing on motorcycles from the early 1950s and had a series of custom leather outfits made for her to ride in every weather condition. For racing, she designed a one-piece leather suit with a diagonal zipper across the chest and contracted the German leather firm Harro to make it. Images of AEG banked over on her BMW R69 soon made a global impact. She wrote for magazines about racing, especially women's racing, and her articles could be found in print around the world in the early 1960s, from Sweden to Tokyo and even in *Cycle World*.

Goldmann was over 6 feet tall, utterly charming, beautiful, and a fierce competitor on the track. She loved racing above all else and endured abuse from both her family and racing men in the early 1950s because a woman racing in postwar Germany was unthinkable. Attitudes towards her softened as she the press attention "legitimized" her. Still she was denied a

racing license in Europe because she was a woman and was relegated to "women's races" and regularity events. She was a feminist and founding supporter of the Women's International Motorcycle Association (WIMA) and had a great many famous friends and admirers with whom she corresponded regularly.

One of those correspondents was French writer André Pieyre de Mandiargues, who wrote the 1963 novel *La Motocyclette*. It features a beautiful young woman, Rebecca, who rides her Harley-Davidson from Strasbourg to Heidelberg for a tryst with a former lover, leaving her sleeping husband in bed on her dawn escape. Rebecca's ride becomes an erotic frenzy as the vibration from her big twin brings her to orgasm, and, in her distraction, she crashes and dies. She wears nothing beneath her one-piece leather riding suit, famously "naked under leather," which was the European title of the film made from the book in 1968—also known as *Girl on a Motorcycle,* directed by Jack Cardiff and starring Marianne Faithfull.

It's abundantly clear Anke-Eve Goldmann was the model for Rebecca in *La Motocyclette*. AEG was not interested in being a sexual icon, however, and the eroticization of her image was galling; she soon dropped journalism and effectively disappeared. She was still a café racer fan, though, and rode a Magni-tuned super-hot MV Agusta 750S into the mid-1970s.

one was ridden to second place in the 1969 Isle of Man Production TT. The success of Rickman in the 1960s and beyond was proof that one could build a gorgeous motorcycle that did everything better and charge what you needed to—Rickmans were always stunning and sold in the thousands.

ENTER JAPAN

The first Japanese motorcycle to really make an impression on Western riders was a factory café racer: the Honda CB92. Despite its diminutive 125cc size, it provided a 70-plus miles per hour top speed, was stone reliable, and had really cool styling. Buyers could order a range of racing kit parts directly from the factory, including a tachometer, bump-stop seat, long curved carburetor bell mouths, and rearsets. The same kit of parts, plus a five-speed gearbox set, was available for the next remarkable Honda, the CB72/CB77 Super Hawk. The CB77 nudged 100 miles per hour and put fear into the hearts of British manufacturers, which were in no position to offer an inexpensive OHC vertical twin that did not leak, could be revved hard all day, and had an electric starter and reliable lights. In the United States and Britain, there was lingering resentment against Japanese products post–World War II, but Honda's "nicest people" marketing campaign won over nonriders to adopt two wheels and led to the largest motorcycle sales boom in history. Sadly that boom did not include British machines, as their lack of investment in new tooling and new designs suddenly left them as also-rans by the end of the 1960s.

By the time the Honda CB450 twin appeared in 1966, the future of the motorcycle industry was clear: here was a DOHC road bike with peerless technical specification that was totally affordable. The CB450 looked great in its original "Black Bomber" guise, with black paint and chrome tank panels, and it had performance equal in real-world terms to British 650s. Honda got an astonished reception to the CB750 in 1968; it was not a café racer, and compared to the well-developed sporting machines from Britain, Germany, or Italy, its handling was mediocre and brakes were wooden. Its faults would be rectified in the 1970s by café racer chassis suppliers, but its rivals in the late 1960s were a better bet if you wanted to ride hard and look good doing it. The CB750 was

Don Rickman in 1968 rests on a Rickman-Triumph café racer with a tuned Bonneville engine and their own design of Lockheed front disc brake. *HMA*

This 1962 Norton 99SS with a lovely two-tone paint job is entered in a production race and is stocked with the addition of a racing seat and Avon Clubman fairing. *HMA*

still a tour de force from a company that had sought to dominate Grand Prix racing and succeeded in a remarkably short period to win every category of World Championship multiple times.

Other Japanese makes with ready-made café racers included Suzuki, whose Super Six 250cc two-stroke twins were good for nearly 100 miles per hour; its even better T500 Titan (or Cobra) models were remarkably durable and reliable and handled surprisingly well. Suppliers of bodywork kits got busy with the Titan in particular because its good chassis and high speed made it a natural candidate for clip-ons. Kawasaki made a splash with its H1 Mach III two-stroke triples of 500cc, which were no-holds-barred performance machines with horsepower their raison d'être. While their engines were wicked fast, the H1 chassis was inadequate for the urge available, which was delivered in a very narrow powerband, making them wheelie machines par excellence. Yamaha had perhaps the best-balanced motorcycles from Japan with its RD250 and RD350 models, which had excellent handling and brakes and very good power delivery. Their racing cousins, the TD and later TZ series, revolutionized the Grand Prix scene by the early 1970s, being affordable and delivering performance on par with the Italian factory exotica then dominating racing. It's difficult to find a late-1960s Yamaha RD that hasn't been made into a café racer because they were beloved by riders who valued real-world performance over mere reputation and loved to ride fast through the bends.

BIGGER AND BADDER

The 750cc class became the most important engine capacity for café racers in the late 1960s and was first seen on the Royal Enfield Interceptor and Norton Atlas, both of which vibrated badly at speed. Triumph's answer to the nascent horsepower wars was to add a cylinder to its 500cc twins, creating the Trident (and the BSA Rocket III, as the companies had merged). It was complicated to keep running but was a fast and fun sports machine and could be tuned to give an awesome turn of speed. Norton did one better by creating a new chassis for the Atlas engine, rubber-mounting the engine/gearbox/swingarm and calling it the Commando. It was dead smooth with excellent handling and terrific style, and it was the first truly civilized sporting twin from the British industry. Parallel-twin motors could be made larger and faster but could not be made smoother without a total redesign to include counterbalancing shafts. The Commando made such a redesign temporarily unnecessary because it worked so well; it was finally possible to exploit the power of a big parallel twin without shaking the fillings out of your teeth. Adding "Ace" handlebars was all one needed to convert a Commando into a café racer with which a decent rider could blow off just about anything on the road for many

A home-built NorVin in France in 1968, with a Vincent Black Shadow engine in a roadster Norton chassis and BSA front brake. *HMA*

years to come. It was simply amazing how British makers were capable of pulling rabbits from hats, giving old designs a new lease on life and keeping their products relevant.

That included Velocette, whose single-cylinder machines were quirky but beautifully built, with excellent handling and smooth power. Its Clubman model was a hot sports machine with a ton-plus top speed—it had proven itself with a twenty-four-hour stint at 100 miles per hour on the Montlhéry race circuit in 1961, the first motorcycle ever to do so. Two years later, input from American flat-track racers led the factory to offer a racing cylinder head with huge 2-inch inlet valve and 1 ⅜-inch inlet tract for a big GP racing carburetor. The factory wisely assembled all of its race kit parts to create the Thruxton model in 1965, which joined the BSA Gold Star and Norton International as the ultimate single-cylinder café racers. The Thruxton was faster than either, with experienced riders finding 125 miles per hour from their standard machines using the optional Avon nose-cone fairing—as fast as a Dresda or Rickman 650. The Thruxton had it all: sleek looks, clip-ons, rearsets, a bump-stop saddle, a twin-leading-shoe front brake, alloy rims, and a huge carburetor poking upwards at an angle requiring a cutaway at the back of the gas tank. Owners (including your author) found the Thruxton was not a finicky or peaky road racer but a tractable and easy-to-live-with companion that felt like an extension of one's faculties on the road. The Thruxton was an instant cult classic and a winner of many an endurance race in the period, plus the 500cc class of the 1967 Production TT. Continuing demand meant the factory could have carried on hand-building Thruxtons for a discerning clientele, much as Morgan cars survived, but debts from poor investments (the LE, Viceroy, and Vogue models) caught up with the company by 1971.

ABOVE: The first Norton Commandos in 1968 had Fastback styling and Atlas brakes and mufflers but would evolve into ever faster and sexier models. *HMA*

OPPOSITE: In 1968, Triumph gave GP World Champion Giacomo Agostini a specially tuned Trident, with close-ratio gears, a tuned engine, inverted 'bars, and rearsets. *HMA*

RELAX—IT'S ONLY FASHION

The rocker craze was in full swing for most of the 1960s in England, reaching its peak in 1965. The British press sold a lot of newspapers exploiting tales of suicidal teen motorcyclists coming to gruesome ends. Rockers were happy to exaggerate tales of danger and derring-do, as youth tend to, and

ABOVE: The 1960 Navigator Deluxe was Norton's twin-cylinder 350cc middleweight cruiser. It could be tuned for real speed as proven in a race at Silverstone with veteran Norton rider Harold Daniell hitting 101 miles per hour. *HMA*

OPPOSITE: Dave Degens built ready-made Tritons under his Dresda brand and raced them, too, winning the Barcelona 24 Hours race with one in 1965, and in 1970 he won again after adapting to Japanese motors. *PT*

reporters were happy to sensationalize their stories—sex and death are always good copy. But a young clerk in the employ of *Motor Cycle* magazine, Mike Evans, set the record straight in the February 23, 1963, issue:

The myth of the coffee-bar cowboy flourishes as strongly as ever. In our sphere it has been one of the major talking points of the past six or seven years. It came with the juke-box, rock 'n roll and the espresso bar: it shows no sign of fading. But the cowboy, apart from the name, is not an innovation of the present generation—he has been with us since motor bikes first appeared. Our fathers knew him as Promenade Percy or Bypass Bertie. The frequenting of a coffee bar is not the necessary qualification for being branded a cowboy. In the eyes of the judges—that is, the public—the incriminating evidence is (a) leather jacket and jeans and (b) racy-type bike with dropped bars. That they differ from the enthusiasts' norm can surely be accounted for quite rationally in one word—fashion. Youngsters are nothing if not fashionable. And the contention that denim jeans are impracticable or that drop bars are uncomfortable is only a side issue. In motor cycling, as in most things, our actions and clothes are dictated by fashion. Nowadays, much nonsense is written and talked about "'ton-up kids". The phrase has gradually become synonymous with coffee-bar cowboy, and for that matter, with young motorcyclists.

Ace Café regular Cecil Richards grew up in the Caribbean island of Saint Vincent, then moved to London for school. His brown skin brought racist attention in London schools, so he took up boxing, which sorted out his tormentors. His story is otherwise typical for a Rocker: he first rode a Tiger Cub, then graduated to a BSA Super Rocket. He's quoted in Mick Duckworth's excellent book *Ace Times*, saying, "At the Ace I started enjoying life and making some great new friends. They were wild times, with races, police chases

When it arrived in 1962, the Norton Atlas had the best motorcycle chassis in the world and plenty of speed from its mildly tuned 750cc engine. Racers easily coaxed even more power from this classic machine. *HMA*

and license endorsements, but there were good times, too. We were bad in a way, breaking every speed limit and cutting up just about everyone on the road. But we weren't violent, and our only drug was coffee." It should be noted that Duckworth had himself been a café racer builder and rider since the early 1970s, much as the author of this book took up café racers in the 1980s. For some of us, the disease can never be cured.

By 1968, the British rocker scene had begun to change as the American chopper craze impacted motorcycle styles abroad. By the early 1970s, being a rocker was no longer about innocent fun but was tinged with the menace of 1-percenter motorcycle clubs and their associated attitudes, drugs, criminal behavior, and occasional violence. What once had seemed like a threat to public order was eventually seen for what it was: youthful, if dangerous, fun. That didn't mean the café racer scene was dying, though—far from it. What happened next was a change of fashion for the 1970s and, finally, a response from the motorcycle industry to the huge popularity of café racers worldwide.

Lewis Leathers

Having served the riding-gear needs of riders since the 1920s, D. Lewis branched out with several subbrands over the decades, including Aviakit starting in the 1930s and Lewis Leathers in the early 1960s. The D. Lewis Bronx jacket of 1955 was the company's response to the rock 'n' roll craze sweeping Britain and became the emblem of the Rocker movement on two wheels, even though many riders could only afford cheaper PVC jackets. The leather biker jacket had rebounded from D. Lewis's original 1920s design No. 702 into American motor police and biker fashion, returning to Britain with Elvis Presley's rise to global fame. With a side zip and D pocket, their Bronx jacket was visibly similar to the No. 702, with a shorter, belted waist and an all-important expanding back adapted from the Aviakit line. It was, and is, a perfect motorcycle jacket that didn't bind one's arms when leaning forward over clip-on handlebars and looked cool in every situation.

The biker jacket had international appeal, becoming the fashion of choice for rock 'n' roll rebels everywhere, from France's notorious *blousons noirs* to Switzerland's *Halbstarken*. Its universal adoption as the very uniform of 1950s rebellion became an unconscious shorthand for cool that persists to the present day. Fashion houses in need of a little authenticity have reproduced it (at far greater retail expense), and wealthy urbanites put it on to add a shade of badass to their otherwise harmless existence.

The Lewis Leathers brand was created to cater to rockers in the early 1960s, with designs like the Bronx, Brooklyn, and Lightning models offered with accessory kits that included patches and press-on studs. Riders themselves added badges and the occasional painted slogan, although in a more subdued mix in the 1960s than later rocker revivalists in the 1980s onwards, with their organized armies of chromed studs and graphically perfect painted logos. If you're looking at photos of 1960s British rockers, you're very likely looking at a Lewis Leathers jacket.

Wearing a Lewis Leathers jacket and Tiger sticker, a white silk scarf, and a spotted helmet with accessory visor, Dudley Sutton plays Pete in the 1964 film *The Leather Boys*. LL

THE 1970s: FASTER FROM THE FACTORY

In the 1970s, the motorcycle industry woke up. While youth culture was all the news in the 1950s and 1960s, it wasn't until the 1970s that motorcycle factories fully embraced the trends led by young riders. The sexy seventies embraced powerful motorcycles as erotic objects, with full-page glossy magazine ads abandoning the veneer of being the "nicest people" and instead embracing eros as the real reason people buy motorcycles. The 1970s saw nearly every major manufacturer offer a production café racer, models that today are coveted as absolute classics in terms of design and performance, and often in sales figures too. Riders who could not afford a Ducati 750SS or Laverda SFC or MV Agusta 750S modified their machines to suit—whether they were of smaller capacity, the touring version from the same factory, or something from another make entirely—and used the commanding style of factory café racers as their template. While such rider-built café racers had always been the norm, for once, factories were now offering exactly what speed-oriented riders were looking for: uncompromised racers for the road.

THE EUROPEAN CAFÉ

For speed- and competition-mad Italians, the specialized, single-purpose café racer had never required an excuse; it was the mainstay of their industry. While the decade began with factories offering stylish 750cc twin-cylinder Gran Turismos,

OPPOSITE: The Ducati Mike Hailwood Replica celebrated his remarkable 1978 comeback win at the Isle of Man TT, with styling (if not tuning) straight from the factory bikes. *HMA*

ABOVE: The outrageously sexy lines of Fritz Egli's original Egli-Vincent racer that was snuck into the Zurich Motor Show in 1971 and sat on a block of wood! *EM*

BELOW: *Easy Rider* meets the café racer dream for these boys in Belgrade, Yugoslavia, in the early 1970s, when a moped had to fill all roles. *TV*

by 1974 the range leaders were superhot café racers: the legendary Ducati 750SS, Moto Guzzi V7 Sport, and Laverda SFC models. While the SS and SFC were sold as production racers, they were also road legal, and the envy of the world. With gorgeous styling and awesome performance, the Italians led the industry not in sales but in sheer panache.

The MV Agusta 750S, with its four-cylinder 750cc double-overhead-camshaft motor, set the gold standard for a factory café racer, although it was wickedly expensive. In 1973, Kawasaki built the 900cc Z1, which had a greater power output but didn't hold a candle to the MV in handling, and while it was attractive, it was miles behind Count Domenico Agusta's masterpiece in style. The 1970s MV Agusta fours remain among the all-time ultimate factory café racers, despite a strong rivalry from other factories building masterpieces in their own right. The press criticized Italian bikes for poor electrical connectors and bumpy paint, which seemed jealous and peevish; fast riders knew these bikes were perfect for them, built without compromise and focused on performance. The Ducati 750SS and later 900SS models, Laverda twins and triples, and MV Agusta 750s were as gifts from the gods to café racer fans worldwide and deserve their status as immortals among motorcycles.

BMW embraced the café racer trend in 1973 with the R90S. Designed by Hans Muth, it shared a chassis with the ordinary R90 series but was still the company's most stylish machine ever. The 900cc pushrod flat-twin had an abbreviated half fairing, a racing-style seat, and two awesome paint options: Daytona Orange or Silver Smoke. With 67 horsepower and a top speed of 125 miles per hour, this BMW was no slouch, although it would take attention to suspension and engine tuning, and a strut from headstock to swingarm pivot, to make it a street racer on par with an Italian rival. Still, the R90S is another all-time classic factory café racer.

In Switzerland, specialist chassis builder Fritz Egli—a café racer man to his core—adapted his large-tube spine frames to accommodate Japanese two- and four-cylinder engines from every manufacturer. His Egli-Vincent specials won races in the 1960s, but in the 1970s their engines were finally overpowered by

The end of the Rocker era, in 1971 at the Isle of Man TT—an endangered species captured in the wild by photographer Chris Killip. *CK*

ABOVE: The Egli chassis featured in this pair of Egli Honda EVH750s worked just as well for four-cylinder motors as for the Vincent V-twin for which it was originally designed. *EM*

BELOW: Norton's "yellow peril" Commando Production Racer, a café racer hand-built in the factory race shop with stunning performance. *HMA*

Kawasaki's H3 750cc two-stroke triple, with the next year's Z1 being the final nail in the coffin, so Egli framed them up to make them handle, creating a series of awesome machines built with Swiss quality. Demand for his original Vincent café racer continued because he'd a created a timeless machine, a quality his design shares with other café racers such as the BSA Gold Star and Rickman-Triumph. This only proves that if you want to build a motorcycle for the ages, build a café racer! Still, Egli's Japanese-engined specials were always exciting machines, with performance equal to or better than anything on the road.

Friedl Münch built his incredibly expensive four-cylinder Mammuts in limited numbers, which had a reputation as the fastest motorcycles in the world—and the most expensive. His 1200 TTS carried over from the late 1960s relatively unchanged, with its Featherbed-ish frames and massive magnesium drum brakes and cast-magnesium rear wheels, all made by Münch. Every machine was bespoke, using the NSU 1200cc OHC across-the-frame four, which by 1970 produced about 88 horsepower and gave a top speed of around 135 miles per hour. It was the king superbike of the 1970s and cost almost three times a BMW R75/5 ($5,135 in 1970 delivered to the United States, compared to $1,875 for the BMW). In 1973, the 1200 TTS-E was the world's first motorcycle with fuel injection, which boosted the urge to 100 horsepower, and it was a hit, with 130 units produced (of the 478 total Münch Mammuts built). They are perhaps the ultimate cult café racer and all too rarely sighted on the roads.

AMERICAN COFFEE-SHOP RACERS

From the mid-1920s onwards, American sporting motorcycles developed in isolation from the rest of the world. Like the eucalypts dominating Australia, American racers were of a single genus through 1970: the side-valve V-twin. By 1968, the Harley-Davidson KRTT was a miracle of side-valve development, clocking 150 miles per hour on Daytona's banking. The AMA

Bimota SB2

Bimota was founded in 1966, its name a mashup of its three founders: Valerio Bianchi, Giuseppe Morri, Massimo Tamburini. It was then a heating and air conditioning company, but Tamburini was truly bike mad and used company facilities to modify an MV Agusta 600 "Black Pig" roadster with his own race-winning frame, which led to demand for replicas. Tamburini next built the chassis for Walter Villa's Harley-Davidson/Aermacchi World Championship machines. The Bimota HB-series Honda four-cylinder racers and YB-series Yamaha two-stroke racers followed, setting the industry standard for chassis design.

Bimota's first production roadster was the SB2 of 1975, a machine that wholly defines the 1970s café racer, although no other bike of the era was like it. With wildly sensuous, body-conscious curves, it ranks among the sexiest motorcycles ever built. It was also a work of design genius, although like Hedy Lamarr, its overwhelming sex appeal often leads people to overlook its intelligence. The SB2's frame is unique, splitting in half above its Suzuki 850cc DOHC four-cylinder motor, with self-aligning conical couplings giving a twenty-minute total teardown. Its truss frame was the first to wrap tightly around a four-cylinder motor, leaving the cylinder head exposed for maintenance and using the motor as a stressed frame member. The fork's rake and trail were adjustable by eccentrics, and the combined tank/seat unit had quick fittings for lightning-fast removal.

The perfection of the SB2 was noted by the world's motorcycle press, and most of the factory's customers came from Germany (always a hotbed of café racer activity) and Japan. The Kawasaki-based KB1 followed in 1978, an evolution technically but with styling slightly toned down from the expressively exotic SB2. While Bimotas were still stylistically edgier than any big-factory product, they would never again have the audacious 1970s sideburns-and-flares glamour of the SB2.

The 1980 Bimota SB2 was the company's first road bike and remains among the most extravagantly styled café racers ever built, demonstrating how wild the 1980s got. *MA*

ABOVE: "Rides as if on rails" was high praise in the 1970s; here Sepp Arnold demonstrates just that on an Egli-Honda EVH750 for their 1974 catalog. *EM*

OPPOSITE TOP: Catherine ordered her Norton Commando Roadster in 1971 and had a suit made by Dada Leathers in Paris with her own design and color. *TV*

OPPOSITE BOTTOM: The 1975 MV Agusta 750S was an apex motorcycle with an easily tuned Grand Prix–developed engine and achingly beautiful styling. *HMA*

finally changed its rules in 1969, allowing all motorcycles to compete on a level playing field, with 750cc as the premier racing class. That opened the door for BSA/Triumph triples and Honda CB750s to win the most tele-visible road race in the world. The American café racer scene shifted from a small subculture to an industry juggernaut in the 1970s as the largest market for all motorcycles, especially fast ones. Demand for bigger and faster machines was a constant refrain, and after Dick Mann won the 1971 Daytona 200 race on an orange factory-built Honda CR750 racer, many of the hundreds of thousands of CBs in America gained clip-ons and small fairings. Rickman-Triumphs and Rickman-Kawasakis sold in the thousands, as did everything fast and Italian, and America became the premier market for café racers.

The first production motorcycle explicitly named Café Racer came, remarkably, from Harley-Davidson. "Willie G." Davidson was promoted to vice president of styling at H-D in 1968, the year the company was sold to American Machine and Foundry (AMF). He was a lifelong rider and in touch with social trends, and he had already absorbed chopper style with the Super Glide in 1971, a commercial masterstroke. With the café racer scene domi-nating factory attention in the 1970s, Willie G. responded in 1977 with the XLCR, or XL (Sportster) Café Racer. A stylistic masterpiece with a distinctly American spin, the XLCR was a mashup of "foreign" café racer cues—low lines, sports fairing, lean-forward riding position—with purely domestic flat-track parts from the factory's all-conquering XR750 racer. With triple disc brakes, cast-aluminum wheels, two-into-one curved exhaust, and all-black everything, the XLCR is probably the meanest-looking production motorcycle ever built. The angles of its flat-track seat worked perfectly with the chiseled, extralarge fuel tank, with the abbreviated half fairing (cribbed from BMW's R90S) cementing the design as a pure 1970s café racer. Sadly its spec did not include the XR750 racing motor; it was an ordinary Sportster underneath, making it an expensive styling job. The sales total of three thousand XLCRS in two years was considered a failure by H-D, but in context, that was far more sold than Ducati's 900SS or any other celebrated café racer in the same period. Americans embracing the subculture of speed eventually acknowledged the XLCR as one of their own, with an asterisk on performance, and today it's a coveted collector's item.

JAPANESE TEA-HOUSE RACERS

After two decades of cutthroat competition in Japan among dozens of small motorcycle factories, by 1970 there were four survivors: Honda, Kawasaki, Yamaha, and Suzuki. Honda dominated global motorcycle production, selling hundreds of thousands of its CB-series twins and fours. There were no Honda factory café racers in the 1970s, but race-kit parts were available from the factory, and dozens of independent shops sold parts to boost the performance of the CBs and improve their looks.

Kawasaki came closest to building a Japanese factory café racer in the 1970s, as its H1 Mach III two-stroke triple of 1969 was the hairy wild man of the industry, scaring riders who didn't fully embrace the wheelie as a lifestyle option. The company declared its dedication to all-out power in 1972, enlarging the H1 to a full 748cc and 74 horsepower with the H3 Mach IV model, soon dubbed the "widowmaker." It was the machine that finally toppled the Vincent Black Shadow from its "world's fastest production" pedestal in a purple-metal-flake, wheelie-ing, smoking flash. The two-stroke engine was near the end of its rope, and Kawasaki trumped itself with a 900cc DOHC four, the Z1, in 1973, which was even faster than the H3. The Z1 was genuinely stylish, and it was faster and better handling than a Honda, although still too heavy and underbraked. The Z1 motor was the perfect donor for a "frame job," the Rickman-Kawasaki being a popular café take, with

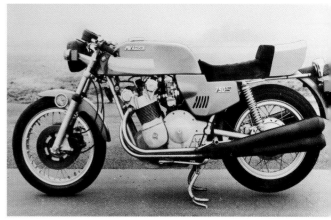

82 horsepower and a top speed of 132 miles per hour, with handling and braking to match and terrific styling.

Yamaha built excellent-handling two-strokes in the early 1970s, and its RD350 was the nearest thing to its all-conquering TZ racer. The RD range was amazingly reliable, simple, and sporty, with excellent handling, and the bikes were immediately drafted into the café racer brigade by the simple addition of Ace bars—all they required, being such a well-designed and amazingly competent machine. Yamaha also produced two future mainstays of the café racer scene in the 1970s: the XS twin-cylinder model of 1970 (a Japanese version of a British vertical twin) and the SR500 OHC single of 1978. The XS-series models, while technically superior, had about the same performance as a touring Triumph 650 and were not widely adopted as café racers until they were rediscovered in the 2000s during the great café racer revival. Both the XS twins and XR singles would be among the most popular and attractive bases for new "Alt.Custom" café racers in the coming age of Bike EXIF, three decades later.

Selling speed with sexual fantasies was common in the 1970s, as with this classic Münch Mammut catalog. *HMA*

1978. THE HORSEPOWER WARS BEGIN: XS11, GS1000, CBX, Z1–RTC

Fierce competition among Japan's Big Four reached a peak in 1978, the year the big guns came out. Honda introduced the amazing six-cylinder CBX Super Sport, with four valves per cylinder and 102 horsepower from 1,047cc. Only Honda could have produced a DOHC six at that moment, although Benelli had beaten them to the six-punch with its 750 and 900 Sei models. The CBX was technically the apex motorcycle of the decade, but it was too heavy to be a café racer—that required an Egli-CBX conversion, which was awe inspiring in its excess.

Suzuki muddled out of its two-stroke past with the GS1000, entering the fray with a DOHC four of its own, which came with mag wheels and triple discs as standard. It could outdrag its CB750F (Honda) and Z1000 (Kawasaki) rivals, and to rub it in, the GS1000 was the first Japanese four with good handling, due to the attention of frame designer Hisashi Morikawa. Suzuki won the Daytona Superbike race in 1978, and in 1979 offered a Wes Cooley replica—GS1000SN, looking very much like the Superbike winner in white with sky-blue flashes, half fairing as standard equipment. The Wes Cooley Suzuki was perhaps the first proper Japanese café racer of the 1970s.

The single-cylinder version of Ducati's 750 Sport, the 1974 450 Desmo, was a perfectly proportioned masterpiece of design. *HMA*

Yamaha's first-ever four-cylinder road bike, the XS11 of 1978, was heavy and powerful at 1,100cc. Despite its shaft final drive and weight of 602 pounds, it could turn a quarter mile in under twelve seconds, and did shockingly well in endurance racing. Kawasaki ended the decade with yet more outrageousness, the Z1-RTC, a beast with the world's first production turbocharger. The 1978 Z1-R had the industry's first sports fairing as standard, proving once again that small-shop café racer builders were always two steps ahead of the industry. The first shots fired in 1978 began years of horsepower wars among Japanese manufacturers and would lead to the wholesale adoption of all-enveloping plastic bodywork as the industry dove head-first into speed. New terms were invented for the café racer, with sportbike and superbike dominating the conversation, but these new-generation machines, while technically amazing, still fed the same old impulse for a racer on the road or café racer.

GHOSTS OF THE ACE CAFÉ

The lion that was the British Empire was nearly on its last roar in the 1970s, as every motorcycle factory went bankrupt or was sold. Chassis builders such as Rickman moved with the times, building superior-handling chassis for Japanese engines. The 1970s were a golden era for chassis builders, before the horsepower wars forced manufacturers to upgrade their frames, suspension, and brakes. Production of Rickman-Triumph twins continued in the 1970s and peaked with their incredible Rickman-Triumph-Weslake eight-valve, 70-horsepower, 150-mile-per-hour masterpiece. A stalled shipment of Royal Enfield 750cc Interceptor engines led to 138 beautifully made Rickman-Interceptor café racers, but the Rickman CR and CRE (Endurance) chassis kits were the future: the first "CR750" Rickman-Hondas proved popular, weighed 100 pounds less than the CB750, and looked great. Plus, losing a "ton" of weight had major performance implications! The Rickman-Kawasaki Z1 900CR was equally popular and considerably faster, and for a time it was the hottest café racer anywhere, with the world's fastest production motor in a lighter and far more competent chassis. It also, in true café racer tradition, was among the best-looking motorcycles of the era.

Industrial designer Rene Adda (Lexon) aboard the wheelie king, the 1972 Kawasaki H2 750 triple, a machine designed for power above all. *RA*

Triumph banked on the Trident model in the 1970s, and while it was faster and handled better than the Honda CB750, it was far more difficult to keep running properly. But a well-maintained T150 or T160 Trident would leave most other machines in the dust, especially with readily available tuning parts inside. For the ultimate Trident, one could follow the factory's lead and install the motor in a Rob North chassis, for the ultimate Triumph of the 1970s. The twins got better with the T140 750cc, which by 1976 gained a front disc brake and other improvements, making it the most robust and reliable of all Triumph twins. By 1976 one could buy a Kawasaki Z1 for the same

price as a T140, and Triumphs became retro, a beloved icon that would not return to contemporary relevance until the 1990s, under a new owner.

ABOVE: Laverda evolved from small singles to big twins and bigger triples, like this 1976 1000 3CL with bull-like performance and macho styling. *HMA*

Norton was in the best shape of the British industry in the 1970s, and the company's sole remaining model, the Commando, held its own for most of the decade, with low weight, great handling, and plenty of power. A factory café racer version of the Commando appeared in 1970, the Production Racer, a race-shop build with lights. With fiberglass bodywork, the all-yellow CPR weighed 400 pounds and was good for 131 miles per hour, briefly making it the fastest road-legal motorcycle in the world. It came stock with alloy rims,

BELOW: Street races were always an illegal but popular pastime. Here Austin Johnson pits his fast Harley-Davidson against a Kawasaki Z-1R in New Jersey. *AJ*

clip-ons, rearsets, a half fairing and solo bump-stop seat, and disc brake up front. It matched high performance with excellent looks, although at $1,900 (about 50 percent more than a stock Commando), it was expensive—but worth every penny, as each machine was built in the factory race shop, with bigger valves and carbs, high-comp pistons, and racing 3S cams. The Yellow Peril, as it was known, was the real deal. Slightly less real, although no less good looking, was the John Player Norton, a factory café racer in the more typical sense of being primarily a styling exercise. In common with Ducati's Mike Hailwood replica, it was an instant collectible, but only the factory version was raced, as the JPN replica was heavier and slower than a standard Commando, with no special tuning.

The café racer scene in England changed dramatically after the release of *Easy Rider* in 1969, and the Rocker scene died out. Youth culture moved on, but performance-oriented riders carried on modifying their machines for speed and style. Café racers were more popular than ever: they had been named and recognized thanks to the Rockers, and the industry had followed their lead. Throughout the 1970s, factories built amazing café racers, and specialist motorcycle builders did a steady business making street racers, which today are coveted as the most beautiful motorcycles of the era.

OPPOSITE: The 1972 Ducati 750 Sport is a premier example of a 1970s factory café racer delivering exceptionally beautiful lines with brilliant performance, stable handling, and mechanical reliability. *PT*

BELOW: While an ordinary Commando under its factory racing livery, the John Player Norton was a classic factory café racer in 1974. *NC*

THE 1980s: RETRO ROCKERS VERSUS PLASTIC SPORT BIKES

A mix of influences in the 1970s had profound implications for café racer culture in the 1980s, transforming what had been a fleeting subcultural identity in the 1950s into a fixed genre within a broader motorcycle culture. The hangover from a lingering 1960s drug culture and the glossy, equally drug-fueled disco era gave rise to twin reactions: 1950s nostalgia and punk rock. The 1973 film *American Graffiti*, featuring small-town California hot-rod culture in 1962, was an enormous hit and a career launcher for director George Lucas (who would release the first *Star Wars* film four years later). It also spawned a wave of extremely popular 1950s-themed nostalgia media, including the musical *Grease* and TV shows such as *Happy Days*. Inevitably, these included characters that embodied the biker trope, giving new life to imagery from 1953's *The Wild One* and reviving interest in the leather biker jacket as a fashion phenomenon.

Magazines such as *Classic Bike* (1978) and *The Classic Motorcycle* (1981) also surfed the nostalgia wave, extending the trend to publishing. Later in the decade, magazines in France, Germany, Italy, and the United States also focused on older motorcycles and associated motorcycle cultures via firsthand anecdotal reporting and important historical research. The popularity of these magazines (*Classic*

OPPOSITE: Fritz Egli built some of the hottest café racers in the world using every kind of engine in his famous chassis, from singles and fours to twins like this Ducati 900SS motor, making an exotic, expensive, and very fast special. *HMA*

ABOVE; The radical 1981 Suzuki Katana grew out of an MV Agusta study by Hans Muth and Target Design and was wisely taken up as a production design by Suzuki. *HMA*

RIGHT: Bimota dominated the dreams of café racer fans with bikes like the SB3 that offered uncompromised quality, perfect handling, and industry-leading speed. *HMA*

Bike circulation reached 350,000 in 2007), which reached worldwide, had an enormous impact on motorcycle culture generally and café racer culture in particular. Old motorcycles rapidly rose in value, and a collector's market created opportunities for dealers, auction houses, owners' clubs, and makers of replica parts for long-dead brands or long-ago models from existing brands. Old-bike magazines raised awareness for a generation of younger riders who'd never seen 1960s café racers such as BSA Gold Stars, Tritons, Bonnevilles, and Dominators or read stories of antics from earlier generations. They provided both inspiration and education, as riders established a subcultural identity, an awareness of history, and self-awareness as inheritors of the mantle of youth culture.

These magazines, and excellent early books on the subject such as Mike Clay's *Café Racers* (1988) and Johnny Stuart's *Rockers* (1987), became style guides for revivalists. From 1984 onwards, Rocker Reunion runs in London and clubs such as the 59 Club and its Classic Section were dominated by note-perfect re-creations or restorations of historic café racers and rocker clothing styles, with a fan base of both graying former original Rockers and new fans. The Rocker scene had become entirely socially acceptable, the grime of the original 1950s rockers polished away in the mirror-like aluminum engine cases of a freshly built Triton. In the 1980s, the most stalwart enthusiasts of café racer and rocker culture began to define "rules" for these historic styles in an effort to preserve their historical integrity.

As the shadow image of rose-hued nostalgia, 1970s punk culture also incorporated the leather biker jacket, as psychic armor for a physically vulnerable and reviled subculture. In the tradition of British Rockers, the jacket was also a convenient billboard to display one's band (or brand) affiliations and an object for DIY decoration: painted or sewn-on imagery, embellished with a postwar American invention, the press-on stud. The influence of punk, the most vital musical genre for Anglo youth culture in the late 1970s and a hotbed of graphic innovation and fashion invention, was enormous and lasting.

The new generation 1980 Ducati Pantah 500SL was light and quick, and it formed the basis of all Ducati's later racing and production successes. *HMA*

Like the nostalgic media, punk, too, led to a new generation of café racer fans. Whether by osmosis or an aha moment, punks discovering historical café racer photos recognized Rockers as kindred spirits, with their shared outcast status and reverence for the leather jacket. In the late 1980s, post-punk, tongue-in-cheek café racer clubs sprang up independently in London (Mean Fuckers), Paris

(Triton Club de Paris), and San Francisco (Roadholders and British Death Fleet), decades before the internet and social media made such international cross-pollination common. Many of these club members and their associates "grew up" to be moto-culture industry fixtures: the Mean Fuckers included Matt Davis (cofounder of *DiCE* magazine with Dean Micetich), painter Conrad Leach, Ben Part (cofounder of *Sideburn* magazine) and Prosper Keating (editor at *Fast Classics* magazine), and their orbit included Mark Wilsmore, who would revive the Ace Café London in the 1990s. The Roadholders included Dr. Robin Tuluie (currently head of R&D at Ducati MotoGP), Adam Fisher (Ace Café San Francisco, 1987–1995), and the author of the book in your hands.

These punk/Rocker clubs were not slavishly devoted to historic styles, and as such they often rubbed older, preservation-oriented café racer fans the wrong way. Ben Part complained, "I was berated by a 59 Club Classic Section member for wearing a pudding basin [helmet] on a 1970s [Moto] Guzzi. 'You shouldn't wear *that* riding *that*,' I was told." Prosper Keating was also invited to join the 59 Club, as long as he "accepted some advice on the wardrobe. They weren't fucking kidding!" This was the classic case of youth culture refusing to submit to the rules of the older generation, which is the essence of punk and the same as the 1950s rockers pissing off the Clubman racers, the Boozefighters MC messing up a 1947 AMA race in Hollister and establishing the "outlaw" trope, or the Promenade Percys "making motorcyclists look bad" to seaside tourists. We can follow this thread all the way back to Sylvester Roper, who no doubt faced tremendous opposition for his steam velocipede in 1869, a horse scarer if ever there was one. Despite ever-adapting capitalism catering to youth culture's

From X6 to RG500 Gamma, Suzuki built amazing two-strokes, and this 1985 four-cylinder hotrod brought Grand Prix technology to the streets. *HMA*

every whim, offering motorcycles, parts, clothing, accessories, and media to suit, the honest creators and re-creators of fast-motorcycle subcultures were never acceptable to the organizing bodies, the squares, or the Man.

This 1985 Egli-Honda single was styled by Hans Muth of Target Design as a short, aggressive café racer single and an update of the BSA Gold Star lineage. *EM*

THE REVIVAL OF CAFÉ RACER COMMERCE

Demand for cutting-edge, performance-oriented motorcycles and parts sustained both large brands and small producers such as Rickman and Bimota, and the revived café racer scene followed the same pattern, with new owners buying historic brands (sometimes at rock-bottom prices) to cater to new interest in old styles. The classic racing scene emerged in the 1980s, leading to the creation of an industry to supply replica parts and even whole motorcycles to this expensive hobby. This had a knock-on effect for builders of vintage-style café racers, with brands such as Rickman, Egli, and Seeley changing hands or licensing production of their older designs to younger,

Bosōzōku

Much like the term café racer, the word *bĐsĐzoku* was a description for teenage speed tribes in Japan, applied by police in the 1950s to gangs of young motorcyclists who roamed city streets, blocked traffic, made noise, and occasionally destroyed property. There was an active café racer culture in Japan from the 1960s onwards as prosperity rose and riders could afford large and fast motorcycles. In the 1970s a peculiar strain of fast bikes emerged with a mixed bag of visual cues for both their riders' outfits and their motorcycles. BĐsĐzoku bikes combined café racer style with chopper cues, including high-mounted race fairings, chopper-esque sissy-bar seats, and Mod scooter lights and accessories. The result was a unique custom motorcycle genre that became increasingly idiosyncratic over the 1970s and saw its heyday in the 1980s. BĐsĐzoku motorcycles typically had serious speed tuning parts installed, loudly announced with race-shop stickers. With their extravagant fairings, huge seat backs, and wind-catching accessories, they were wild-style expressions of a youth moto-subculture. As such, they're kin to other obnoxious rider groups (Promenade Percys, Rockers, et al) complained about for generations.

Photo credit: SC36

enthusiastic small manufacturers. This kept brands alive, often beyond the lifespan of their original creators, as the motorcycle industry as a whole expanded to include historically based brands.

Avant-trend Japanese hipsters brought new life to old motorcycle gear brands such as Lewis Leathers in the 1980s with their reverence for and attention to the minute details of historic designs. Demand for scarce original vintage jackets led to the revival of long-gone lines, for which there were often no remaining patterns; riding fashions had changed dramatically since the 1960s and the old patterns has been discarded. In the case of Lewis Leathers, it took years of dedicated effort by Derek Harris, who brokered the brand's vintage designs to Japanese retro retailers, to collect, archive, and re-create patterns from vintage Lewis, D. Lewis, and Aviakit gear. His efforts were rewarded with the keys to the factory in the 2000s, and the company remains a stalwart of traditional British riding-gear styles. Other brands, such as Schott and Red Wing, licensed their vintage designs to Japanese manufacturers, which have in turn become coveted in the companies' home countries, where these fantastic "heritage" styles are unavailable by licensing restrictions.

The 1980s thus saw a new phenomenon: the rise of retro style as a major part of the motorcycle (and automotive and fashion) industry. Western culture as a whole seemed to lose its taste for the future and turn instead to the past as its happy place, in a conservative backlash against the relentless, dramatic, and constant change of twentieth-century technology. It's difficult to ascribe such a massive trend to changes in the motorcycle industry, but it's equally difficult to deny that the dominant motorcycles of the 1980s were perhaps the least inspiring of the century.

In general, high-performance motorcycles started the decade as massive, powerful machines with deficient handling and ended it as sophisticated and extremely competent but entirely encased in plastic bodywork. Streamlining trends, which designers had toyed with in 1960s and 1970s café racers, now became the dominant style for factory café racers. In every previous generation, the engine and architecture of a motorcycle had been critical components of its overall styling, and a beautiful engine was considered a design imperative. As the 1980s progressed, the near-universality of across-the-frame four-cylinder designs created a boring homogeneity,

Roadholders MC member and physics student at University of California, Berkeley in 1985, Dr. Robin Tuluie went from racing his daily-rider Norton Commando to winning four F1 World Championships as a chief designer for the Renault and Mercedes-Benz teams. *RT*

with the last truly beautiful four being the first produced for the street, the MV Agusta 750. Hiding uninspiring four-cylinder engines behind plastic panels was no great loss, aesthetically, but a barrier between rider and machine led to a kind of alienation: the heart of the motorcycle was unseen, and many riders felt motorcycles had become appliances rather than erotically charged, dangerous, and thrilling companions. It's no wonder an increasing number of riders turned to older machines. By the 2010s, retro-styled motorcycles would become their companies' biggest sellers.

SPORTBIKES AND SUPERBIKES

The tremendous popularity of café racers in the 1970s led to a decade of classic, factory-built café racers, generally labeled as sportbikes. Slim, svelte, and naked, these machines defined the era with razor-sharp styling and were instant classics, especially those from Britain, Germany, and Italy. As we entered the 1980s, however, all that slimness went pear-shaped: the 1980s began with bigger-must-be-better bikes from Japan, as the horsepower wars gained momentum, and outright top speed became the goal, rather than a balance of performance with reasonable weight and excellent handling. The class of 1981 included the Suzuki GSX1100 (1981), Kawasaki GPZ1100 (1981), and Honda CB1100R, all of which pushed the top-speed envelope into 140-mile-per-hour turf and finally began to address the notorious handling issues of 1970s Japanese bikes. The Superbike racing series had a positive influence, as factories were forced to invest in chassis development, and

BELOW: The scene at 4 a.m. on Easter Sunday, 1988 during the annual Easter Ride to the top of Mount Tamalpais for sunrise featured a mix of vintage machinery as the B.D.F. and Roadholders left the Ace Café. *TV*

OPPOSITE TOP: From left to right, Chris Dopp, Neil Hamilton, the Ace Café's Adam Fisher, author Paul d'Orléans, and Richie Rosen take a break during the Japanese brand Nicole Club's fashion photo shoot in 1988. *TV*

OPPOSITE BOTTOM: Pudding basin helmet, Stadium goggles, and a painted jacket for ton up girl Denise Leitzel, one of the Roadholders MC, in 1988. *AS*

1980s sportbikes reaped the benefit. They were still gaining weight, though, with all the machines squashing the scale at 550 pounds.

Yamaha built the best Japanese factory café racer of the era, and one of the best of any era, with its two-stroke RD350LC (1981). While the motor-cycle press flipped out for More! Power!, the RD line was already per-fected. With a superb frame cribbed from Colin Seeley's notebook (plus a monoshock swingarm from the TZ racers) and a water-cooled 350cc motor making 47 horsepower, the RD350LC would hit a "modest" 110 miles per hour (nearly as fast as a Norton Commando, anyway) but tipped the scales at a dainty 310 pounds. No, it wouldn't do 140, but some riders didn't fancy hauling an extra 250 pounds of weight around corners.

Making a two-stroke twin equal the big fours in performance took Grand Prix technology, and in 1984 Yamaha offered the RD500LC, which took on an extra 80 pounds of weight in exchange for a top speed boost of 30 miles per hour, to 138 miles per hour, right up there with the (very) big boys that had over twice the engine capacity. This outrageous little machine with GP-level performance still weighed less than 400 pounds and boasted the industry's best suspension, handling, and brakes on a street bike—a real racer on the road, the textbook definition of a café racer. The owners of such machines bucked the trends of the day and recognized themselves as "real riders" who enjoyed usable road performance and the sheer joy of bend-swinging over

ABOVE: The scene outside San Francisco's Ace Café in 1989, with a Suzuki GT750 "kettle" converted to café racer spec. *TV*

OPPOSITE TOP: d'Orléans with Josiah Leet on the top of Mount Tamalpais in 1988, with two jackets painted by the former in an extrapolation of Rocker style. *TV*

OPPOSITE BOTTOM: Fashion meets the punk/Rocker scene. Supermodel Linda Evangelista poses with the Mean Fuckers MC in London during a Peter Lindbergh photo shoot for *Vogue*. *PK*

an ego massage for being an owner of "the fastest," regardless of the limited possibility of exploiting a machine's full potential anywhere but on the racetrack. Then again, plenty of owners took their RDs to the track and did very well. Japanese manufacturers produced masterpieces in the 1980s, such as Suzuki's GSX-R750/1100 and Honda's unexpectedly beautiful RC30 (VFR750R), which somehow managed the miracle of telegraphing its speed potential and overall balance in the design itself despite being entirely clad in plastic. The RC30 was a rare thing, an instant classic, and a devastating track machine. Very few were used on the road, as they were expensive, and many who kept them off the track kept them in their living rooms instead!

Amazingly, a second American factory café racer appeared at the end of the decade, when Erik Buell began series production of his RS1200, which used Harley-Davidson's 1,200cc Sportster engine. With a modest 60 horsepower, the RS1200 was good for "only" 120 miles per hour, although Buell's race-derived chassis and streamlined half fairing gave performance far in excess of the Sportster, and handling in a totally different league. With an underslung monoshock and light trellis frame, the Buell was also 50 pounds lighter than a stock H-D. It was a genuine performance machine for riders who wanted to move fast around corners. BMW reentered the sportbike market in 1989 with its only-in-the-'80s K1. With total plastic bodywork enclosure and bold graphics, the K1 was BMW's first 100-horsepower machine, fast enough (at 145 miles per hour) to be relevant in the speed-obsessed 1980s but too heavy (at 570 pounds) to give racer-like handling. Its styling was not for everyone, and it was certainly too heavy-looking to be considered a café racer—unless one handed it to California tuning shop Luftmeister, who, for a substantial fee, would sharpen up the suspension and add a turbocharger to give 160 horsepower at the rear wheel and an industry-leading top speed of 185 miles per hour.

While Ducati went through big changes in the 1980s, the factory still produced exquisite street racers from 1983 onwards using Dr. Fabio Taglioni's final engine design, the Pantah. The smaller 500cc Pantah models won the European F2 racing championship four years running (1981–1984), and, similar to Yamaha's RD350, they made light roadsters with perfectly balanced performance. All this was improved in 1985 with the 750cc F1 models, which had trellis frames built of short, straight tubes that provided a radical visual appeal and remain the signature of Ducati chassis to this day. The F1 design is minimal and slightly brutal in its functionality, with a purity of purpose as a superhot street racer, built to look as light as it weighs, with little compromise for the street. Continuing with its brand identity as a builder of factory café racers, Ducati reintroduced the 900SS

line in 1989, giving affordable real-world road performance, ease of maintenance, and genuine riding pleasure. It was a gift to the motorcycling
world and a very big seller for the firm, as it turned out there were plenty
or riders who thought 135 miles per hour was good enough, if one could
actually use all the performance available. Like most Ducatis, it delivered
sensual pleasures when cracking open the throttle for a basso profundo
exhaust note, and the broad spread of midrange power made two cylinders
far easier to ride fast than a screaming four-cylinder mill.

Ducati upped the ante in 1989 with the 851, which proved the foundation for the next generation of their road and racing efforts. With a water-
cooled eight-valve engine producing 104 horsepower and a low weight of
396 pounds, the 851 electrified the sportbike world with its great looks
married to very high performance and the intoxicating cadence to its riding sensations. Rather than a shrill buzz from a 14,000-rpm four-cylinder
engine, the 851 loped along, producing big power all over the rev range
with a fantastic exhaust note like a NASCAR racer. Proving that lighter
and better handling could triumph over sheer horsepower, the 851 took

three consecutive World Superbike championships. The riding position was uncompromising for taller riders, as this was truly a racer on the road, built for a full-time racing crouch.

Bimota entered the 1980s with its second roadster, the HB2, based on the twin-cam Honda CB900F. The HB2, with its exotic tube-and-aluminum-plate frame, was 70 pounds lighter than its donor Honda, with premium magnesium Ceriani wheels and fork sliders, fully adjustable forks front and rear, and Brembo triple disc racing brakes. With a long half fairing and one-piece tank/seat unit, the styling was pure racer, and its chassis showed the way forward for the industry. Within three years, every manufacturer offered full fairings as standard, although none could match the quality of Bimota's build or its incredible mix of low weight and GP handling. For a big four, its 440-pound weight was by far the lowest of any Japanese four-stroke sportbike, but such attention to quality and performance did not come cheap: Bimotas were exquisite café racers, but they were always a wealthy person's toy. The company's next trick was a leap forward in sophistication, the YB6 EXUP (1989). The YB6, with power from the Yamaha FZR1000 EXUP, had full plastic enclosure, which could be forgiven, as (1) it was beautifully shaped, and (2) it was the fastest production motorcycle in the world. Lightning fast, and handling as if secured by magnets to the earth, the YB6 used the first twin-spar aluminum frame in the industry, which helped with handling and kept the weight down to a remarkable 407 pounds. It's no wonder the racing version (YB4 EI) won the 1987 Formula 1 World Championship. While the YB4 proved that lightness was a worthy and achievable goal, it also steered the industry towards total bodywork enclosure as a guiding principle.

With factories catering so explicitly to café racer fans in production as well as press, the flavor of motorcycling itself had changed by the end of the decade. Few in the industry were asking, "How fast do we need to go?" With no end point in sight, the answer was always "Faster!" But the peak years of the 1980s would soon shift into decades of falling sales, sometimes precipitously slipping, which raises the question: Was the focus on ever-larger, more plastic-covered, heavier, and faster machines ultimately alienating to new riders? Or did cultural forces change the perception of motorcycles as a "necessity" for young riders to express their independence? Did the rich urban bikers and weekend warriors of the 1980s kill authentic moto-rebellion?

OPPOSITE TOP LEFT: Though the original Ace Café in London had since become a tire shop, café racer fans Adam Fisher and Bill Stone built their own Ace Café in San Francisco to pay homage to the original biker meetup. Your author's Velocette Thruxton takes its place of honor. *TV*

OPPOSITE TOP RIGHT: The punk/Rocker scene of the 1980s brought a new generation of café racer fans together, like Wendy Fish and her Panther with a matching jacket painted by your author. *PdO*

OPPOSITE BOTTOM: Members of the punk/rocker café racer club the Mean Fuckers MC of London pose on a warm day at the end of a Brighton beach run. Pearl, Rob Carr, Johnny Campling, Prosper Keating, Matt Davis, David Lancaster, and Jake Turner. *PK*

THE 1990s: ALL PLASTIC EVERYTHING

Two parallel developments in the café racer scene defined the 1990s: "hyperbikes" and the retro movement. Ordinary riders could finally purchase Grand Prix technology for the street, as the gap between road and race had closed. The hyperbike was everything a café racer enthusiast wanted, in theory. But what happens when the motorcycle you've dreamed of becomes commonplace, and its performance exceeds your ability to use it? That's an existential question, and one that motorcycle manufacturers began to grapple with in the 1990s, as sales of new motorcycles slumped despite the machines themselves having reached an awesome state of development.

As the ultimate example of "racing improves the breed," performance motorcycles by the 1990s incorporated the lessons of Grand Prix and Superbike racing. With late-1980s superlatives such as the Honda RC30 as glowing examples of possibility, the general trend across the industry was to lighten sports machines and improve their handling and braking using ever-better components. "Ladder" frames made of short, straight tubing, or perimeter frames in cast aluminum, became the new gold standard. The development of suspension components and tire technology, the arrival of excellent frame designs, and the advancement of engine-tuning knowledge made hyper-sport bikes the norm in the 1990s. Japanese and Italian factories, especially, offered

OPPOSITE: The 1990s saw performance coalesce into extremely rideable hyper café racers, like this 1999 Yamaha YZF-R6, a shockingly competent, 430-pound, 600cc beast with 150 miles per hour on tap. *AS*

The Harley-Davidson Sportster engine has fine qualities, and specialist builders revisited its café racer possibilities in the '90s in machines such as this Hans Muth-styled Egli. *EM*

incredible café racers, whose performance exceeded the abilities of the average street rider. The motorcycle press entered a feedback loop that encouraged more performance, with highly skilled riders testing new bikes on racetracks as if racing were the goal of all riders. The motorcycle press had changed since the 1970s, with the introduction of post–Hunter S. Thompson gonzo reportage, with *BIKE* magazine the prime example in the United Kingdom. Professional distance was replaced by exclamation-point hyperactivity, in a circular dance with advertisers that made real criticism rare and discouraged such existential questions as "What the hell is happening with sports motorcycles?"

Wisdom typically comes in retrospect, and from a distance of over twenty years now, it's clear to see the early signs of the motorcycle industry's loss of relevance to youth culture in the 1990s. Hyperbikes were the fruit of a century's search for perfect motorcycle performance, but what then? While there's always room for change, improvement, and new directions, the successful pursuit of performance above all had created a machine more akin to a fast-moving appliance than the throbbing, visceral animal it had been for a century. Simply put, much as we curse them for needing our attention, we have a personal relationship with motorcycles when they need a little love, but we take what is perfect for granted. One may become attached to a motorcycle-appliance (which I refer to as the second-most intimate of machines, after the vibrator), but that attachment is to the riding experience, not the vehicle itself. For a century, riders had loved both the experience *and* the motorcycle, which goes a long way to explain why many café racer fans turned their interest toward vintage bikes—or, if artistically inclined, towards homemade or creative alternatives to factory designs. While moto-artistic trends had their origins in the late 1940s, the 1990s sowed the seeds for a completely new scene that exploded in the 2000s as motorcyclists voted with their feet, walking out of the dealerships and back into their garages.

STREETFIGHTERS

A new strain of café racer emerged in the late 1980s as an alternative to the classic 1960s-style adaptations of four-cylinder Japanese machines. The name streetfighter was popularized in the United Kingdom, but the style appeared in the rest of Europe and in the United States as well, where the style was called, among other things, the rat bike. In time-honored fashion, the recipe was simple: take a cheap and well-used high-performance motorcycle, strip off the plastic bodywork, and perhaps spray-paint the whole machine matte black. Typical additions included

Ducati's 1992 900SS Superlight had carbon fiber touches and proved so popular that Ducati built 900 of them. The half-fairing was penned by Monster designer Miguel Galluzzi. *NC*

Patrick Godet

He was a bear of a man whose fanatical love for Vincent motorcycles lasted over forty years and developed to the point of manufacturing the amazing Godet-Egli-Vincent specials for which he became famous. At his small factory in Malaunay, just outside Rouen in Normandy, France, Patrick Godet built over 250 of his beautiful Vincent specials—and repaired or restored countless original Vincents and engines for owners around the world—with incredibly high standards. The Godet Vincent reproduction engine could be ordered up to 1,330cc, with double the horsepower of the original, and was built to cure many of the known faults of the 1940s Vincent design.

Patrick Godet purchased his first Vincent, a Black Shadow, in 1974, and soon bought a Black Prince as well. The lure of racing caught him in 1979, when the French vintage racing scene was founded; he tuned a Black Shadow to Lightning spec and was formidable in French historic racing. He further developed the machine to take on the British vintage racing scene as well, with veteran racer Hubert Rigal at the helm. The pair won the 1985 Vintage Race of the Year with the Vincent Spéciale.

Godet turned to Fritz Egli's chassis to upgrade the potential of the Vincent engine and approached the master for permission to reproduce the EV frame. On seeing the quality of Godet's work, Egli agreed to make him the only licensed manufacturer of the Egli frame, and the Godet-Egli-Vincent was born. It was an ultimate café racer, especially with one of the new 1,330cc engines, which brought performance into modern territory with simply exquisite aesthetics. The GEVs were built in a new factory by a team of six by 2006, and the waiting list for new machines was very long indeed. By the time of his death in 2018, Godet had been building Vincent twins far longer than the Vincent factory ever did. His café racers were among the best ever made.

In the 2000s, a Patrick Godet–built Egli Vincent with a special oversized motor was about as sexy as a retro-café racer could be. *MW*

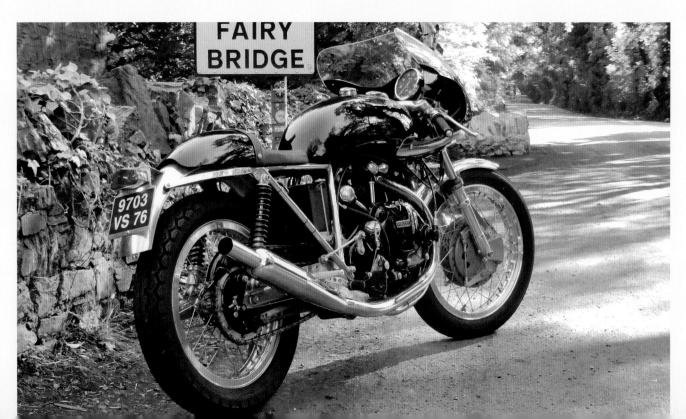

performance exhaust systems (Muzzy, SuperTrapp, Kerker) and, for the more ambitious, newer suspension and brake components to improve handling. Streetfighters were often created from 1980s or 1990s sportbikes that had crashed, with their plastic bodywork destroyed; replacement panels were expensive, so riders simply left them off, adding cosmetic touches to make the appearance palatable. It was the oldest story in motorcycling: young riders making do with what they could afford, adapting their secondhand bikes to suit their taste and budget, and inventing a new style in the process.

Or, in the case of streetfighters, a kind of antistyle, more akin to a Mad Max stunt bike than the glittering café racers of the retro Rocker scene. Nevertheless, their focus on performance made them part of the café racer family, although traditionalists (now that there were such for café racers) were loath to accept them as such. Just as with all café racer scenes through history, the streetfighter crowd developed their own related riding gear, hangouts, slang, and media, with the style's number-one print exponent being the United Kingdom's *Back Street Heroes* magazine.

Ducati carries on as it always has—a builder of factory café racers since day one. Massimo Tamburini's design for the 1994 748 made one forget it was plastic. *HMA*

OPPOSITE: Royal Enfield is India's smallest moto-builder, but it dwarfs European and American factories. Fritz Egli turned their venerable Bullet into a café racer in 1992. *EM*

LEFT: More a dragster than a café racer, the Yamaha V-Max proved so popular it was reintroduced twice; this 1993 model is used as the maker intended by Ed Cheney. *AS*

Streetfighter gatherings had a soundtrack of aggressive hard rock and death metal, with a macho, Mad Max–esque style of riding gear and streetwear, all complementing the rawness of their motorcycles, which exposed the unfinished, not-meant-to-be-seen engine castings and chassis details normally hidden under plastic. The streetfighter style, with its rejection of the all-plastic-everything motorcycles, had an important impact on industrial motorcycle design. It was a stylistic protest against plastic motorcycles, and the industry took note, creating what was then a shocking return to a basic motorcycle profile, sans bodywork, which became known as the "naked" bike.

THE MONSTER

Designer Miguel Galluzzi was the first in the industry to address a growing distaste for all-enclosing plastic bodywork. He consulted for Honda from 1987 but wasn't happy with industry design trends: "I was working on the Honda CB600F2, and it was all this plastic crap covering everything up." Ducati hired him in to develop the new-generation 900SS, which came fully faired and was a big success, becoming the brand's number-one seller. Still, Galluzzi wanted to see the bodywork trimmed; he cut the bodywork down on his personal 1987 Ducati 750 Sport to demonstrate how less plastic could be more appealing,

Alan Sputhe tuned his road-legal Harley-Davidson Sportster for 157 miles per hour in 1978 and sold tuning parts and whole engines, as with this 1994 Big Twin with 125 horsepower. *AS*

and at the 1990 Bologna Motor Show, the factory revealed a 900SS with an abbreviated fairing. "That was the beginning of the changes," he told me. His first "naked" bike was an 851-powered prototype, but the new four-valve engine was expensive; the factory had plenty of the 900SS motors in stock, so that became the basis of the M900 model, which Galluzzi dubbed the Monster, after his children's favorite toys.

The response to the Monster was a collective industry-wide gasp at its radical simplicity. This reaction seemed absurd to fans of café racers, streetfighters, and vintage motorcycles, for whom two wheels had always been "naked," and even Galluzzi was surprised how difficult it was to move the needle in motorcycle design back to traditional forms. "People said 'this is extremely futuristic', and I said, have you been looking at bikes from 50 or 60 years ago? To me it wasn't radical, it was just going back to basics." The Monster, of course, became Ducati's biggest seller, remained in production for decades, and changed the course of the motorcycle industry. Within a few years, every factory would offer naked, streetfighter-ish models with no or minimal bodywork, returning motorcycles to their roots.

RETRO CAFÉ RACERS

The retro café racer scene became surprisingly popular in the 1990s. London's Ace Café had closed in 1969, becoming a tire shop, but it still held its appeal as a mecca for café racers, as the name was still resonant. Stories from the 1950s inspired a "new" Ace Café in San Francisco in 1987 as an homage to the long-gone original in London. The first Ace Café Reunion event in London was organized in 1994 by Mark Wilsmore, and it attracted an estimated twelve thousand people, which encouraged Wilsmore to take on financial partners to reopen the original Ace Café in 1997. The nostalgia movement, begun in the early 1980s, had come to full fruition as a simultaneous celebration of past and present-day Rocker culture, with a significant emphasis on café racer motorcycles.

The revved-up interest in vintage café racers was good news to specialist parts suppliers and to vintage motorcycle dealers and auctions. All aspects of the vintage motorcycle industry rose on this tide of interest, and companies such as Davida supplied them with period-correct helmets and other gear. David Fiddaman had founded Davida in his mother's garage, making box-section swingarms for café racers in the early 1980s. They were well built and an easy swap to cure handling issues with powerful Japanese fours and included an eccentric-cam chain adjustment system, just like a Bimota. Fiddaman (or Fid the Lid) noted that old pudding-basin helmets were much in demand by the retro Rocker crowd, as well as with vintage racing enthusiasts, so he began building high-quality replicas of old helmet brands as the first Davida helmets. They proved popular in Europe, Japan, and the United States, but while great looking, they were not legal, sold strictly on an "at your own risk" basis . . . which was, in truth, a tremendous risk, and some enthusiasts paid the ultimate price for fashion. Fiddaman therefore developed a new line of jet helmets in the 1960s style, which were also handmade in England and beautifully finished—and fully legal. Davida was for many years the only helmet manufacturer in England, and the brand's jet helmets have been fully certified in every country, which is rare even for the biggest helmet makers. Other boutique helmet manufacturers followed in the 2000s, including Ruby and Hedon.

By 1993, the Honda CBR900RR was everything one could want regarding performance and reliability. It was a Superbike for the street, if you liked all-plastic-everything. *AS*

THE DENIM REVIVAL

The global spread of the heritage and vintage clothing craze after the rise of nostalgia media in the 1980s meant traditional clothing brands rediscovered their older styles in the 1990s. Revivalists held up a mirror to these brands by reminding them how cool and evergreen were their own designs of the 1950s–1970s. Japanese enthusiasts were at the forefront of both the retro Rocker and retro café racer trends, with vintage-style body kits available for bikes such as the Yamaha SR500 and newly made leather jackets and denim trousers produced in the old style by small companies. Levi's had moved some denim production to Japan in the 1950s to take advantage of lower labor costs, but small mills that made denim from raw cotton in both the United States and Japan began to close in the 1980s, and as with other manufacturers—of clothing, motorcycle gear, and motorcycles themselves—Levi's was at first unaware on the burgeoning vintage clothing movement that revered its older styles. New companies sprang up to meet the increasing demand in the 1990s for authentic styles, and some, especially in Japan, took out licenses from old brands to recreate so-called heritage styles, which were exactingly true to original 1930s–1960s designs of jeans, boots, or jackets, and a whole new industry of Japanese denim was born. Some heritage styles were copies of classic designs, while others used them as springboards for new designs inspired by the past.

The heritage style movement began as a fascination with older motorcycle styles in Japan and had a knock-on effect with "cool hunters" in the rest

Rocker-inspired café racer clubs like the East Bay Rats popped up around the world in the 1990s as the punk/ Rocker scene of the '80s grew. *AS*

Derek Harris

The rise of the Rocker revival in the late 1980s was part of a widespread trend of revivalism around the world. A subculture of revivalists may have been spurred by nostalgia in popular media, but these groups were pioneering enthusiasts of the past whose deep and detailed knowledge of vintage clothing gave rise by 2000 to a new industry of heritage clothing and accessory manufacture. Demand for authentic, high-quality vintage gear sometimes boomeranged to the very companies whose past products enthusiasts sought out, with Levi's being perhaps the primary example, reintroducing classic designs under the Levi's Vintage label.

Lewis Leathers sold very good and functional motorcycle clothing during the 1980s and 1990s, but something of its stylistic essence had been lost; the new products, for example, had extra seams and used black polyester lining instead of quilted red sailcloth. Bright colors had been introduced in the late 1960s to coincide with the advent, in the United Kingdom, of color TV, which meant racers could be spotted by their suits instead of by race number, and in time-worn fashion this became a trend with street bikers. Derek Harris began sourcing Lewis Leather jackets in 1991 for a Japanese rock-fashion clothing store, noticing the developing market for heritage items at the time. Harris explains:

I suggested to Lewis Leathers owner Richard Lyon that we should try accurately recreating the old styles. At the time, LL was virtually unknown in Japan, but a growing scene of riders interested in vintage British bikes naturally drew them to LL and its UK styling. Their licensed Japanese distributor wasn't particularly effective promoting Lewis Leathers in the country, and thus a demand for vintage & second hand Lewis jackets evolved.

Demand from Japanese vintage dealers for authentic Lewis Leathers designs from the 1950s–1970s led Harris to liaise directly with the company starting in 1991 to re-create their back catalog. "The Japanese shops wanted vintage styles, but the original patterns had all been lost. I began buying any old D. Lewis, Aviakit, and Lewis Leathers styles I could find, and hired a pattern maker so Lewis Leathers could make them again," he said. The new Lewis Leathers jackets were as accurate to the originals as they could be, including the correct zipper and snap manufacturers, the right labels, and correct polyester fabrics for their quilted lining.

Derek Harris became an archivist extraordinaire for this single subject, spending twenty-five years pulling together the intellectual property for this 125-year old company, and he wasn't even an employee but a broker for Japanese dealers. That changed in 2003, however, when the owner of Lewis Leathers informed him he intended to sell the business and retire, but said, "Don't worry—I've found the perfect new owner." A shocked Harris responded "Who?!," only to be informed it was he who was the only rightful heir of the brand. Though gobsmacked, Harris nonetheless gathered the necessary financial support to buy the brand and opened the first Lewis Leathers retail store in twenty years, at 3–5 Whitfield Street, not far from the original D. Lewis location in central London. It has the flavor of the 1960s store, with racks of fantastic leather designs, plus Harris's amazing collection of original Rocker jackets and memorabilia, giving the shop a priceless and impossible to replica patina of authenticity.

of the world. In the 1990s, Japanese-language motorcycle magazines revealed a professional side of the vintage café racer scene that was not yet extant elsewhere. The Japanese scene included a focus on heritage style gear that brought companies such as Lewis Leathers and Davida new energy. Heritage style was part of a cultural mix brewing up something new in the late 1990s, which would blossom in the 2000s with the related "neo-custom" or "Alt.Custom" motorcycle scene. This mix felt new and exciting as a self-conscious embrace of historically cool elements, recombined to create a contemporary mashup. And, for the first time since the 1970s, the heritage scene attracted young non-riders to motorcycles—bikes were becoming cool again, with profound influences on the café racer scene and on the motorcycle industry as a whole.

SUPERBIKES BECOME HYPERBIKES

In the 1990s, motorcycle manufacturers were obsessed with café racers as the leading edge of the industry. This was the same as it ever was—the fastest bikes making headlines—although the industry felt compelled to call them something new again; while the 1980s brought us sportbikes and superbikes, the 1990s delivered hyperbikes. These were machines of breathtaking performance that became amazingly balanced over the decade, with huge horsepower ratings matched by incredible brakes, suspension, and chassis designs. The 1990s was launched by the Kawasaki ZX-11 with its 176-mile-per-hour top speed, which was the first response to Honda's magnificent RC30 in combining huge horsepower with excellent handling. It was perhaps the world's first hyperbike, but the term wasn't extant yet. The ZX-11's meteoric speed was created with no regard to production racing regulations: it was assumed that the motorcycles being world's fastest would be sufficient to sell them, without track dominance.

Yamaha responded with big improvements to their FZR1000 model, introducing GP-style upside-down forks for the first time on a production motorcycle, which honed the handling to a beautiful pitch. Changes in suspension technology were the story of the decade, but these were matched by improvements in tire technology, which made better handling possible. Honda reacted to the renewed horsepower wars with the CBR900RR in 1992, which had an even more highly tuned engine and a presumed natural home on the racetrack—hence the Road Race (RR) suffix.

The nostalgia market propelled Lewis Leathers to new success and a revitalized lineup as global demand for authentic period designs grew in the 1990s. *LL*

Honda had proved capable of bringing its track prowess to the street with the RC30, and the CBR900RR carried on that legacy, being compact and relatively lightweight, with exceptional handling to match its swift power delivery. Suzuki revamped its GSX-R750 in 1996, making it lighter and faster than the 1980s original, with wicked acceleration and razor handling made possible by the loss of further pounds.

Ducati fans, perhaps the truest café racer cadre of all, were delighted with the introduction of the 916 model in 1994, with its water-cooled, bigger-capacity four-valve engine. The power of its new L-twin motor gave a top speed nearly equal to its four-cylinder rivals, but Ducati's strong suit has always been the drivability of its engines, which delivered more power at lower revs than its neurotic four-cylinder competition. Ducatis sounded much better too, unleashing a deep basso profundo aria at the twist of the wrist. Best of all was their bodywork, sketched out by Massimo Tamburini, which was breathtaking in its timeless modernity, suggesting speed from a standstill. The 916 defined "horny," looking lean and mean, and could be forgiven its total plastic enclosure for being so absolutely gorgeous. It remains a legend, a worthy stablemate in the pantheon of all-time great factory café racers, alongside the BSA Gold Star, Ducati 750 Sport, and Honda RC30.

Two more Japanese bikes vied for best-of-honors for the 1990s: the Yamaha R1 and Suzuki Hayabusa. The R1 was everything the decade was seeking, an easy-to-ride rocket ship with amazing handling, making a

Harley-Davidson tried its hand at international-level road racing with the VR1000 project and built the 1993 VR1000 roadster as a homologation special. *AS*

ABOVE: The rise of nostalgia culture brought attention to historic design, inspiring new customs with vintage style. Andy Saunders rides J. Regers's road-legal Honda CBX café racer remodeled in '60s factory GP livery. *AS*

OPPOSITE: Former Harley-Davidson factory race mechanic Steve Storz sells tuning parts and whole bikes to make Sportster café racers like this 1993 hot rod. *AS*

better rider of an owner who pushed its tires hard. The Hayabusa became the king of the horsepower wars for the decade, with 160 horsepower and a top speed of 194 miles per hour, which any American sixteen-year-old could buy with a learner's permit. The 200-mile-per-hour barrier loomed remarkably close, and would be broken in the next decade, but it began to finally give pause to the nearly all-male club of motorcycle journalists normally pickled in a testo-erotic steam bath inside their full leathers. How fast was too fast? The question has never yet been seriously posed by the industry, with even the Germans abandoning their voluntary 100-horsepower limit in the late 1980s, under pressure to stay relevant as the projectiles flew in the never-ending horsepower wars. But it was answered by the public in the late 1990s and 2000s, as buyers, or rather nonbuyers, voted with their feet: the industry was clueless about what ordinary people wanted. It would take outside forces to bring sanity back to the industry, not to mention a sense of fun, rather than manic speed obsession. Fun and cool would return to motorcycles in another decade, but dark years remained, and big questions not yet pondered in the 1990s would come to dominate the conversation, including the relevance of the internal combustion engine itself.

10

THE 2000s: THE INTERNET CAFÉ IN THE TWENTY-FIRST CENTURY

The rise of the Internet was the best thing that ever happened to café racers, although traditionalists did not necessarily agree! The sudden wealth of image-sharing websites, blogs, and social media platforms spread the ultracool appeal of classic café racer photos from the 1950s, 1960s, and 1970s to a new generation that had never subscribed to *Classic Bike*. In fact, many of these new enthusiasts had never owned a motorcycle and were exactly the demographic the motorcycle industry most needed to reach—new riders—but it took a surprisingly long time for the industry to respond.

The rise of motorcycle websites spawned a third wave of café racer revivalism, along with a totally new take on the genre, using models that had never previously been fodder for speed modification, with details and a hybridization of styles that had never been seen before. The new, post-internet café racer scene was not part of the postpunk scene of the 1980s and 1990s, or any musical scene, but was certainly promoted by the veterans of the 1990s café racer scene through media. Its fans were as young and impecunious as their forbears, and they intuitively followed their internal compasses toward their own true north: what was cool.

OPPOSITE: Walt Siegl builds limited-edition café racers, usually around Ducatis like this Leggero, with improved performance and simply superb aesthetics. *CM*

ABOVE: A pioneer of the new custom scene in the early 2000s, Chicara Nagata's impeccable work around a racing Meguro engine for the Chicara III pointed a new way forward for café racers. *CN*

OPPOSITE TOP: Ian Barry established himself as a man to watch with his Falcon Motorcycles customs in 2009, and his Vincent-based Black was the machine we'd been waiting for—simply amazing. *FM*

OPPOSITE BOTTOM: Shinya Kimura built customs in Japan with Zero Engineering before moving to Los Angeles to do his own thing, like this amazing MV Agusta 750 Sport with futuristic bodywork. *PS*

In the early 2000s, the motorcycle world was a strange place, with the scene split between factory-built hyperbikes, heavy cruisers, and—the most visible of all—fat-tire choppers, built on TV for shows such as *Biker Build-Off* and *Monster Garage*. While reality TV shows made several builders into stars, viewers were not necessarily inclined to buy choppers on the strength of a TV appearance. Worse, motorcycles as a whole seemed to have become boring to young people, and sales of new bikes to riders under forty were dropping like a stone. One writer at the *New York Times* even asked "Are Motorcycles Over?," pondering whether bikes had ceased to be sexy enough, and rebellious enough, for a new generation of youth. Yes, bikes are always dangerous (and will be until self-driving technology takes inattentive car drivers out of the motorcycle-death equation), but they were no longer a rite of passage of youth, and it showed: biker gatherings in the 2000s looked like a mob of ageing pirates, with so much gray weekend stubble and do-rags on display.

The café racer had gone, once again, underground, but a new generation would soon discover the simple beauty of the racer on the road. Young people hotly followed the growing number of early motorcycle blogs, including my own blog The Vintagent. And just like in every era of motorcycling, they started building café racers once again, looking at the classic examples from history, and making their own café racers using the cheapest bikes available that had inherent style (mostly 1960s and 1970s Japanese machines). As BSA Gold Stars and Velocette Thruxtons were far out of reach financially for motorcycle newbies, the Yamaha SR500 became the universally desired big single to transform into a street-racer lookalike. As Triumph, Norton,

Chicara Nagata won the American Motorcycle Dealer World Championship with this Harley-Davidson Model U–based custom in 2006, alerting the world to the Japanese custom scene. *CN*

and BSA twins were likewise out of reach, and notoriously difficult to keep running, we saw the rise of "CB customs," based on Honda CB350, 450, and 750 models—typically with plank seats, low bars, and no mudguards at all, in this new iteration of the café racer style. The chorus of doubters decried their hard seats and lack of rain protection, but style was all what mattered to this new generation of builders. These bikes were the new cool.

The global financial crisis of 2009 changed motorcycling radically, and the ashes of the TV custom motorcycle scene proved fertile ground for new ideas. The previous generation of custom bikes, dominated by fat-tire choppers and reality TV motorcycle shows of the early 2000s, lost their appeal or went out of business entirely when the economy crashed. Turn-of-the-century customs had become baroque, overly concerned with a flashy finish and stuck in a V-twin lineage popularized after the release of *Easy Rider*. Forty years later, busted banks killed the post-*Easy* custom scene as the leading edge of independent motorcycle design.

Deus Ex Machina

If one company sums up the Alt.Custom scene and its impact on contemporary café racers, it's the Australian brand Deus Ex Machina. With its mix of surf, skate, and motorcycle culture framed in distinctive branding and graphic work—the design genius of Carby Tuckwell—Deus exploded worldwide as the apex of cool style, even (perhaps especially) for folks who'd never ridden, surfed, or skated. Dare Jennings founded the brand in 2005 in Sydney after selling his ultrasuccessful anti-establishment surfwear label Mambo for A$20 million in 2000. Dare was a motorcyclist as well as a surfer and skater, and he pivoted that successful formula to incorporate all of his interests at once, with an emphasis on moto culture.

Dare had seen the first flowerings of the Alt.Custom scene while visiting Japan in the early 2000s and understood intuitively that something new was afoot. While the motorcycle industry overall was catering to a shrinking cadre of older riders, he saw in Japan the beginnings of something new for motorcycles, with the same potential for independent, young, and fun scene he'd surfed with Mambo. The first Deus Ex Machina "Temple of Enthusiasm" opened in a warehouse in the low-key Sydney suburb of Camperdown. At the time, its mix of motorcycles on the floor, surfboards, racks of clothing and tee shirts, books on shelves and art on the walls, and a café, was simply unheard of. It was lifestyle branding at its finest, and Dare opened sister outposts in Venice Beach, Milan, and Bali that all shared the formula as emporiums of a cool, indie style. Each location included a custom motorcycle shop, where the output was mostly café racers, built from a mix of vintage Japanese singles, twins, and fours, plus a few more contemporary donors from Triumph, Kawasaki, MV Agusta, and others. Basically anything they fancied turning into a café racer was fair game.

The typical Deus café racer fits squarely in the Alt.Custom mold, with flat seats, minimal or no fenders, and a clean, light aesthetic, typically achieved by "de-tabbing" the frame (cutting off extraneous fittings). Removing side covers, battery trays, complex electrical systems, and airboxes, gives a motorcycle a spare, light look, much like a purpose-built racing machine from the 1930s. The Deus style is a mix of old aesthetics taken from vintage racers applied to modern machines, with a contemporary twist, in a style that could only have come from the internet age.

Retro or nouveau? The Deus Ago TT by "Woolie" Woolaway references vintage bodywork over a brand new MV Agusta café racer. D

RIGHT AND BELOW: Medaza Cycles, located near Cork, Ireland, believes in riding amazing café racer customs, like their Rondine, built around a Moto Guzzi Falcone Nuovo. *PT*

OPPOSITE: Japan's Cherry's Company is guilty of inspiring lust for their designs around the world, and their BMW-based Highway Fighter was inspired by the BMW's 1930s landspeed bikes. *KT*

What emerged during the Great Recession, though it had already been growing silently in Japan and California, was an alternative custom scene, which your author dubbed the "Alt.Custom" movement in 2009. The new scene was not dependent on V-twin motors, and not so interested in choppers, although choppers were having their own renaissance in the form of a skinny-tire, 1960s-style revival. The Alt.Custom movement grew rapidly from 2005, after a few pioneering Japanese builders, such as Shinya Kimura and Chicara Nagata, came to prominence, crafting handmade café racers that stretched the genre into the realm of fine art. Other builders followed suit, including the Wrenchmonkees in Denmark and Falcon Motorcycles in Los Angeles. By the time the Bike EXIF website was founded in 2008, there were enough new customs in a mostly café racer style for a daily feed of global Alt.Customs. Bike builders were seemingly interested in every kind of custom or racing motorcycle tradition besides choppers: café racers, scramblers, dragsters, 1910s board-track racers, 1930s hillclimbers, ice racers, speedway bikes, Japanese bōsōzoku gang bikes,

ABOVE AND OPPOSITE: Kengo Kimura's shop Heiwa Motorcycle in Hiroshima produces gem-like customs like the *Dirty Pigeon*. Built around a 1971 Triumph TR6 motor, it's a surgically clean style that betters factory practice. By adding additional upper frame rails, Kimura created horizontal lines that unify his design while emphasizing horizontality which reads as speed. *KM*

and on and on. Every shape or configuration ever used on two wheels was fair game and worth exploring. Suddenly the emphasis of a young scene mixed a bit of history with a fun, no-rules aesthetic.

That piqued the interest of a motorcycle historian—me—who saw hope for the future of motorcycling in this new embrace of its past. With young artists and builders looking at old motorcycles for inspiration, suddenly the job of a historian had a fresh breath of life and a new audience of young, intelligent minds unburdened by the nostalgia and the old brand loyalties of traditional collector-historians. The kids liked old bikes because they looked cool, and that was enough. This was motorcycling from an entirely fresh perspective. It was incredibly exciting to recognize its origin and watch the scene grow into a global phenomenon, with a related explosion of creativity in writing, photography, filmmaking, and fashion, all interconnected and generating fresh energy from mutual inspiration. Speaking as a historian of motorcycles and motorcycle culture, it seems clear we've entered a new cycle of artist and builder engagement with the motorcycle—the most exciting since the 1970s.

Motorcycles are most emphatically not over, although the American, Japanese, and European big-bike industries are still suffering. Regardless, their most popular new models have been inspired and popularized by the Alt.Custom scene: the Triumph Thruxton and Bobber, the Ducati Scrambler, the BMW R nine T and its Scrambler and Café Racer variants, the Royal Enfield Continental GT, and others.

LEGENDS OF THE MOTORCYCLE

One of the first physical encounters of American enthusiasts with the new style of Alt.Custom machines was at the Legend of the Motorcycle Concours d'Elegance of 2006–2008. This was the first Concours to include custom motorcycles, and the foresight of event producers Jared Zaugg and Brooke Roner cannot be overstated. The Legends show brought together historians, collectors, industry heavyweights, and custom-bike stars the world over, and the 2006 exhibit was the first time most Americans had seen the work

Falcon Motorcycles reimagined a Velocette Thruxton as if Brâncuşi had designed it, with *Bird in Space* curves and amazing attention to detail. *FM*

of Shinya Kimura in person. Sat beside the work of chopper TV superstars such as Jesse James, Kimura's bricolage café racers using Triumph, Harley-Davidson, and vintage Excelsior power were hand-wrought and sculptural, and they lacked the gloss of the overweight metalflake behemoths on display around them. They suggested totally new possibilities for the café racer genre.

The Legends Concours introduced many future Alt.Custom café racer stars to one another and the world, including Ian Barry of Falcon Motorcycles and Vincent Prat of Southsiders MC, who escorted Daniel Delfour's Norton Ala'Verde to the 2008 Legends. This led to an invitation to your author to ride in Biarritz in June 2009, establishing an annual ride that grew in 2011 to include David Borras of El Solitario MC as well as Fred Jourden and Hugo Jézégabel of Blitz Motorcycles in Paris. The next year that ride was codified into the Wheels and Waves festival in Biarritz, which took its place among the many influential and ultracool weekend motorcycle shows around the world that reinvigorated the café racer scene.

ABOVE: The Vincent Black Shadow is an evergreen café racer inspiration, and New York's Keino Sasaki nailed the genre with his Widow Jane hot rod. *RH*

LEFT: Ronin Motorworks built a limited edition of 47 machines around the Buell 1190RX including this one, *Oishi Yoshiro*, for a run at the Pike's Peak Hillclimb, where it came second. *RM*

The launch of the Ago TT at a "temple of enthusiasm," the Deus ex Machina emporium in Venice, California, where coffee meets surf meets skate and motorbike. *D*

THE RISE OF THE ALT.CUSTOM SHOW

Dare Jennings, who founded Deus Ex Machina in 2005, was among the first to respond to the Japanese trends, creating a new, fun, and very hip counter-culture opposing the American chopper scene. As Deus's visual brand identity spread around the world, it seemed somehow connected with the new Brooklyn hipster culture, as both shared a fascination with vintage or heritage clothing, rampant facial hair, denim, and a cheeky retro graphic aesthetic. Motorcycles were a big part of the equation, and by 2009, specialized shows of new-generation customs and café racers appeared in the two hotbeds of American hipsterism: Brooklyn and Portland. The Brooklyn Invitational had more of a chopper bent but always included café racers, while Oregon's One Moto Show tended to include more street scramblers and café racers. Neither was huge compared to the American Motorcycle Dealer shows and other traditional motorcycle events, with their tens of thousands of visitors, but they were critical poles to a new generation of café racer enthusiasts.

The impact of the Brooklyn Invitational and One Show among cool hunters was extensive, leading led to a wave of new custom motorcycle shows—and builders to fill them with bikes—in the 2010s. The list is long and includes Born Free, Mama Tried, the Handbuilt Motorcycle Show, Wheels and Waves, and the Bike Shed.

ALL MAKES, ALL BIKES

The most popular bikes to café racer–ize in this period were among the cheapest available, including Honda CB series twins and fours, Yamaha XS vertical twins, and the Yamaha SR400/SR500 single, which, amazingly, has remained in production since 1978. Among the most iconic version of the new-style café racer SR500 came from Deus, whose ultrasimplified "Grievous Angel" in all-black everything captured what was best about the new scene: it wasn't slavishly chained to the past, and it looked clean and relatively easy to build. As in all works of genius, the Grievous Angel also seemed to have been latent in the original SR500 design, only requiring a talented sculptor (in this case, Michael "Woolie" Woolaway) to "release it from the raw stone," as Rodin said. Hundreds of copies were made—a few by Deus themselves, but most by do-it-yourselfers inspired by the perfection of the Deus bike.

The Honda CB series from the 1970s was the most popular basis for café racer conversion in the 2000s, as they were ubiquitous, cheap, and reliable. Every variant was included, starting with the flat-single C100 model, which is still in production under license in Asia, and with literally tens of millions of C100 examples available, it formed the basis for a wave of inventive café racers from Vietnam, Indonesia, and Thailand. The 305

A new generation of talented artisans, such as Raccia Motorcycle's Mike LaFountain with his re-creation of a Kawasaki W1R racer, reaches to the past for inspiration. *MLF*

Kenny Cummings builds exquisitely crafted updates on Seeley-framed café racers under his NYC Norton brand. A 1007cc Norton Commando motor propels this Streetfighter Seeley, a 300 pound ballerina with a heavyweight boxer's punch. *ML*

Super Hawk, which had always been a popular café racer conversion, was revived in new, stripped-down forms—as was the CB450 in all variants, right up to the CB750, which got a boost from the Dutch brand Wrench-monkees with the perfection of its Gorilla Punch, which established an entirely new branch of the Alt.Custom café racer tree.

Two-strokes from Yamaha and Kawasaki were also fair game, and the possibilities for sculptural expansion chambers inspired many builders, with notable builds from See See Motorcycles (Thor Drake) and from Roland Sands Design, whose all-aluminum RD/RZ brought out the original racer-on-the-road brief by mixing genuine road-race parts from Sands's career as a number-one AMA champion with a few road-legal parts to make a kick-ass café two-stroke that would have been welcome in any era. While two-strokes were virtually banned for sale in the United States, original examples were perfectly acceptable on the road, and with no oppressive government oversight on modifications, it was possible to radically alter, for example, a Kawasaki Mach III triple for truly mind-bending road performance.

In India, an expanding middle class and overall increase in wealth made the first custom/café racer scene in that country emerge, called chai racers by some in Mumbai. The basis of these machines was invariably a Royal Enfield Bullet or a license-built Jawa two-stroke, and although any modification of motorcycles is forbidden by law in India, lax enforcement has allowed for a burgeoning café racer industry, which was led by commissions from wealthy Indians, including Bollywood movie stars wanting a slice of the new cool.

IMPACT ON THE INDUSTRY

Like a beacon of fun, the new generation of independent customizers guided the big manufacturers out of a generation of funk. Street scramblers and café racers became the most popular over-the-counter styles, as the factories successfully poached the energy of this new scene: the new models inspired by millennial customizers proved, naturally, to be their most popular models. Royal Enfield responded to the new global café racer craze, and its Indian counterpart, by re-creating one of the most iconic factory café racers of the 1960s, the Continental GT. The new GT was built around the 500cc Bullet platform with disc brakes and successfully captured the look and spirit of the original—it's a perfect retro café racer with its original proportions and style intact, making Royal Enfield the only modern factory to convincingly reintroduce an old model.

Every other factory building modern-day versions of old models has ended up with a very different animal, as most bikes have become larger and heavier over the decades. Thus the new Triumph Bonneville—though it has a charm all its own—is a much heavier beast than the original, with scaled-up components to match, and lacks the feminine delicacy of Edward Turner's designs. Still, the Bonneville is Triumph's most popular model once again, and for good reason—it looks terrific, and owners found it very easy to modify as a café racer. The factory took note of all these DIY custom café racers and offered its own in 2004: the Thruxton model, a proper café racer with low handlebars and a humped rear seat.

As mentioned, sales of the usual hypersportbikes and heavy tourers were dropping, but the new Alt.Custom and café racer scenes provided a breath

of fresh air, pumping new blood into the industry and restoring motorcycles' status as cool. Are motorcycles necessary as a rite of passage for young people again? That question still lingers for the motorcycle industry as a whole, but one thing remains certain: there will always be a group of preening, speed-crazed, distinctively dressed youngsters who find the lure of the café racer irresistible. The size of that subculture has grown and shrunk over the past century, and there's no reason to doubt that the next generation of motorcycles—the electric café racer—will be just as exciting as with every past decade. Looking over the whole history of motorcycles, and beyond into the age of bicycles and horses, it really does appear that café racers are forever.

OPPOSITE AND ABOVE: The reborn Brough Superior SS101 combines retro cues like George Brough's iconic 1920s plated saddle tank with an up-to-date 120 horsepower 88deg V-twin motor from Boxer Design in Toulouse, France, where the new machine is built in limited quantities for wealthy customers, just like the original. *BP*

EPILOGUE:
THE BLUE SPARK OF THE FUTURE

As much as we love the rumble and roar of a finely tuned engine, it's very likely our relationship with the internal combustion (IC) engine will change in the near future. Urban centers are already banning IC vehicles, including those in China, where three million electric scooters are whizzing through the streets, and Oslo, which will soon allow only electric vehicles. The implications for urban fans of café racers are clear: things are going to change, likely through legislation, and the days of pouring gasoline into a motorcycle, except as a novelty, are numbered.

The electric café racer is an idea whose time has arrived, but it has been slow in coming. There are sound technical reasons for this, mostly due to battery and controller technology languishing for 150 years, after the first electric motorcycle design was patented in 1869 by Louis-Guillaume Perreaux. Nothing but golf-cart performance could come of repurposed car batteries and car starter motors powering a motorcycle chassis, which describes basically all electric motorcycles until the mid-1970s. In 1974, Mike Corbin upgraded that combo to a pair of jet-fighter starter motors and a set of Yardney nuclear submarine batteries (with $100,000 worth of stolen US Navy silver bars) to power his Quicksilver up to 201 miles per hour at Bonneville. Corbin was alone in the wilderness, but he'd made his point: there was a fast future coming, and it buzzed rather than burbled.

OPPOSITE: The first electric café racer, the Mission One (2009), was sketched and 3D-printed by design superstar Yves Behar for Mission Motor Company. It boasted a 150-miles-per-hour top speed. *HD*

BELOW: As a first shot across the bow of 100 years of internal-combustion-powered café racer history, the Mission One made its point with avant-garde styling. *HD*

The humble cordless electric drill was the clarion call for the future in the mid-1990s, when a new generation of compact, powerful batteries (NiCad and LiOn) became commercially available. Just because you had more power from better batteries didn't mean you could use it, though, and now a new generation of controllers used to modulate power to an electric motor were needed. As electric motors produce 100 percent of their power from 0 rpm, considerable technical finesse is required to prevent constant burnouts, wheelies, and flips from an e-bike with 50-plus horsepower. It took another decade for a decent, compact controller unit to be developed, and we can thank the car industry (think Tesla) for its huge investment in technical research.

The first electric café racer with performance matching gas-powered bikes was built by ex-Tesla employees in 2008. Operating as Mission Motors, they partnered with industrial-design superstar Yves Béhar to reveal the Mission One, the world's first electric superbike, in 2009. It had 150-mile-per-hour performance but was fiercely expensive, and the first machine built was offered in the 2010 Neiman-Marcus Christmas catalog at $73,000, double the price of the most exotic Italian race replica on the market. The electric motorcycle market developed very slowly, and companies like Mission Motors came and went, as existing motorcyclists weren't particularly interested in electric bikes, and techie early adopters were scared of motorcycles.

OPPOSITE: The fastest production motorcycle in the world in 2016 was American and electric: the Lightning LS-218, which shines an LED light on the future of fast motorcycling. *LM*

BELOW: Customizers are eager to get their hands on electric sports bikes, and DeBolex Engineering made a lovely café racer from an Energica Eva as a promotion for TW Steel and the film *Oil in the Blood*. *TH*

The café racer of the future is free to be whatever a designer intends. As with Untitled Motorcycles' Zero XP, voids are left to be filled with your imagination and a reminder that nothing is permanent. *LR*

It didn't matter to the motorcycling public that the world's oldest racing series at the Isle of Man included an electric TTXGP in 2009, followed by the TT Zero series. These were one-lap races, as although the bikes were fast, they didn't last, and recharging—as opposed to refueling—was an hours-long affair. When the title of world's fastest production motorcycle (however nominal that production may have been) was handed to the Lightning LS-218 in 2014, it should have been front-page news, at least in the motorcycle press, but it barely garnered a sidebar. That the world's fastest street motorcycle was made in the United States should have been included in a State of the Union address, as that hadn't been true in a century, but again, we heard nothing but crickets. The Lightning did catch international press when it trounced all the gas-bike opposition in the Pikes Peak hillclimb in 2013. Short-distance racing is the killer app for e-bikes, as their tremendous torque and acceleration can be exploited to the full, and their endurance is inconsequential.

Today we have a number of electric café racers available over the counter, from low-powered, inexpensive machines from Zero to the sportbike-styled offerings from Energica, but the question remains: will the café racer subculture survive a transition to electric? As we've seen, the subculture of speed on the road is older than motorcycling itself and is more a matter of human nature than any particular technology, period, or style. As people are fundamentally the same over time and adapt quickly to new technologies, there's no doubt the café racer scene will continue in whatever form two wheels takes in the future. Like the faded blue tattoo on an aging Rocker's arm proclaims, it's café racers forever, mate.

ACKNOWLEDGMENTS

My education about café racers began with *Classic Bike* magazine in 1984. A few years later, books like Jonny Stuart's *Rockers* and Mike Clay's *Café Racers* appeared simultaneously with the Punk/Rocker scene of the 1980s, of which I was part. Decades later I discovered that friends like Matt Davis of DiCE, artist Conrad Leach, publisher Prosper Keating, and photographer Ben Part were having the same fun across the Atlantic. Their stories are integrated into my discussion in Chapter 8.

When I founded TheVintagent.com in 2006, I found allies with whom I could share photos and research—authors such as Francois-Marie Dumas, Mick Duckworth, Stefan Knittel, Thomas Trapp; collectors such as Jeff Decker, John Goldman, Dave Clarke, Derek Harris, Richard Ostrander; and people who lived during the era such as Richard Vincent, Rene Adda, etc. Most importantly, the Hockenheim Museum Archive has generously provided space, time, photographs, and friendship and is a peerless resource for serious researchers into motorcycle history and culture.

Thanks to Chris Hunter for writing the Foreword. Thanks to all the café racers I've owned since 1984 for providing endless hours of inspiration and riding pleasure (and a few of heartache). Thanks especially to Susan McLaughlin, for tolerating a man on a mission.

PHOTOGRAPHY CREDITS

This book would not be possible without the photography or photographic collections of the following people and institutions. Each photo in this book is tagged with an abbreviation of its contributor, and the identification key is below:

AC: Ace Café archive
AF: Adam Fedderly
AJ: Austin Johnson
AS: Andy Saunders
BS: Mark Upham
BP: Bill Phelps
CG: Chris Gruzkos
CK: Chris Killip
CM: Craig McDean
CN: Chicara Nagata
D: Deus ex Machina

DC: Dave Clarke collection
EM: Egli Motors archive
FM: Falcon Motorcycles
FMD: Francois-Marie Dumas collection
HD: Hardy Danger
HM: Hockenheim Museum Archive
JD: Jeff Decker collection
JG: John Goldman collection
JVM: Juan F. von Martin collection
KM: Kazuo Matsumoto
KT: Ken Takayanagi
LL: Lewis Leathers archive
LM: Lightning Motorcycles
LR: Ludovic Robert
MA: Mecum Auctions
MLF: Mike LaFountain
MO: Matthew Olson collection
MW: Mars Webster

NC: Nick Cedar
NPG: National Portrait Gallery
NPL: Nostalgia Picture Library
PdO: Paul d'Orléans
PS: Pan Sumi
PT: Philip Tooth
RA: Rene Adda
RH: Ryan Handt
RM: Ronin Motorworks
RO: Richard Ostrander collection
RT: Dr. Robin Tuluie
SMC: Solo Motorcycle Works collection
TH: Tom Horna
TT: Thomas Trapp collection
TV: The Vintagent archive
VMCC: VMCC archive

INDEX